Heroic
M O R M O N
Women

Heroic Mormon Women

Ivan J. Barrett

Covenant Communications, Inc.

To my favorite heroine:
my wife, Minnie

Cover painting *The Pioneer* © Robert T. Barrett

Cover design copyrighted 2000 by Covenant Communications, Inc.

Published by Covenant Communications, Inc.
American Fork, Utah

Printed in the United States of America
First Printing: April 1991

10 09 08 07 06 05 04   12 11 10 9 8 7 6 5 4

ISBN 1-57734-676-9

Contents

A Gallery of Mormon Heroines

"Let Her Own Works Praise Her"

Some years ago a young woman read her great grandmother's journal. Afterward she mused:

I wish I could be close beside you tonight, Grandmother, and have you tell me firsthand of the things I am reading in your journal. You were a young bride when you left your comfortable home in Nauvoo, full of love, life, and romance. I would not want to trade this age for yours, Grandmother, but I wish I might have known, as you did, the Prophet Joseph Smith and might have seen him, as you saw him, astride the fine black horse your father gave him.

"What are you doing with that fine animal?" the Prophet had asked, as he passed your father's pasture in Nauvoo.

"I am training him for you, Sir," said your father, and right then the Prophet left on the shiny black mount, which became a favorite with him.

After the long journey across the plains, did you glimpse a beautiful mirage in Salt Lake Valley when you came down from the mountains? Were you greatly disappointed to find only sunflowers, sage growing here and there, and big black crickets crawling about on the sunbaked earth?

In your day, Grandmother, the only hazard from

the streets was an occasional runaway horse or team, but death rides the highways today. I still say I would not trade my day for yours, but I would barter for some of the peace and quiet of your day that I might tread more surely through the years. I have gained new strength and a faith that will help me to carry on because of those things you told me in your journal.

Great-Grandmother, you are a heroic woman to me and others like you have and will forever inspire us of this later generation. If I only knew more surely my origin and destiny as a woman, I, too, might be heroic and inspiring to generations yet unborn.

As from the voice of the infinite came the words of President John Taylor to the women in his day:

Lady, whence did you come? Your origin? What are you doing here? Where are you going? What is your destiny? Know you not that you are a spark of Deity struck from the fire of His eternal blaze? Know you not that eternities ago your spirit pure and holy dwelt in your Heavenly Father's bosom, and in His presence, and with your mother, one of the queens of heaven, surrounded by your brother and sister spirits in the spirit world, among the Gods?

Your spirit beheld scenes transpire there, and you grew in intelligence, and saw worlds upon worlds organized and peopled with our kindred spirits who took upon them tabernacles, died, were resurrected, and received their exaltation. You longed, you sighed, and you prayed to your Heavenly Father for the time to arrive when you could come to this earth, which had fallen from where it was first organized, near the planet Kolob.

At length the time arrived and you heard the voice of your Father saying, Go, daughter, to yonder lower world, and take upon you a tabernacle, and work out your probation with fear and trembling and rise to exaltation. But daughter, remember you go on this condition, that is, you are to forget all things you ever saw, or knew to be transacted in the spirit world; but you must go and become, while in your infancy, one of the most helpless of all beings that I have created, and will be all your life subject to sickness, pain, tears, mourning, sorrow, and death. But when truth shall touch the cords of your heart, they will vibrate; then intelligence shall illuminate your mind, and shed its lustre in your soul, and you shall begin to understand the things you once knew, to understand and know the object of your creation. Daughter, be faithful as you were in your first estate.

You bade Father, Mother, and all farewell and came on this globe. "Obey my law, choose him you loved in the spirit world to be your companion, and crowns, thrones, exaltations and dominions will be reserved for you in the eternal worlds, and, if faithful, you will be permitted to pass by Gods and angels to your exaltation in the celestial world among the Gods. To be a glory to your husband and offspring, to bear the souls of men to people other worlds, while eternity goes and eternity comes." If you will receive it, lady, this is eternal life. Remember that the man is the head of the woman, and the glory of the man is the woman.

Hence your origin, the object of your ultimate destiny. If faithful, lady, the cup is within your reach, drink then the heavenly draughts and live.[1]

This is your origin and destiny: to learn to be heroic in your own right. Now come with me and view the lives of those heroines of the Church who lived nobly, who lived well and worked out their divine destiny admirably and acceptably before Eternal Providence. In our saga of *Heroic Mormon Women*, we bring to you the gripping yet touching story of Mormon womanhood, "fuller of romance than the works of fiction."[2]

It is my hope that these brief accounts of our sisters will make dearer to our hearts their heroic contribution to the building of God's kingdom in these last days.

History has largely been written by men for men. On the printed page of the past, little space has been given to women. Behind every truly great achievement of a man, there has been a woman; but man, as he has chronicled the events of history, has often forgotten to mention the hand that rocked the cradle. Consequently, the prominence and importance of women in history has not been fully recognized nor appreciated and their potential to inspire modern women remains mostly unfulfilled.

Even writers of our own Church History have not given our sisters the recognition they deserve. In all the events of the thrilling, moving, faith-promoting history of Christ's Church restored upon the earth, the mother, wife, and daughter have been so far in the background as to be seldom mentioned. I am not unmindful, mark you, of the Prophet Joseph Smith's commendatory estimation of the sisters, nor of similar praise of the fairer sex by other leaders even down to our day. I am also not unmindful of the Prophet's organizing of the Female Relief Society which embraced the women of the Church in a wonderful sisterhood.

Yet the history of the Church has been a history of the activities of men. And, in many respects, this is as it should be, for the priesthood is held by the brethren who direct God's affairs among men on the earth. But still, the touching story of the mother at home caring for the little ones while her husband is away preaching the "word," of the fearful anxiety resting upon her for the health and welfare of her little ones, of the struggle to make a living and to take the full responsibility of the family has too often been neglected. This is lamentable, for the records of this great Church of Jesus Christ present "an epic of woman, not in all the ages 'has there been one like unto it.'"[3]

To begin, let us say that all of us owe our very existence to womanhood. Our birth, our training, the care we required in our tender years, we received from our mothers. My own mother was an inspiration to me. My love for the gospel, my urge to pray, my desire to learn, all the inclinations toward the good and the worthwhile, I owe to my mother. We can bring many witnesses to testify that we are heavily indebted to our mothers. The Wizard of Menlo Park, Thomas A. Edison, when once praised for his miraculous achievements, declared: "My mother was the making of me. She was so true, so sure of me; and I felt I had someone to live for, someone I must not disappoint." An old rabbinical proverb says, in effect: "Since God could not be with us always, he gave us mothers."

The writer of Proverbs described the type of woman that many Mormon women exemplify:

> Who can find a virtuous woman? for her price is far above rubies.
> The heart of her husband doth safely trust in her . . .
> She will do him good and not evil all the days of her life. . . .
> Strength and honour are her clothing; and she shall rejoice in time to come.
> She openeth her mouth with wisdom; and in her tongue is the law of kindness.
> She looketh well to the ways of her household, and eateth not the bread of idleness.
> Her children arise up, and call her blessed; her husband also, and he praiseth her.
> Many daughters have done virtuously, but thou excellest them all.
> Favor is deceitful, and beauty is vain: but a woman that feareth the Lord, she shall be praised.
> . . .Let her own works praise her in the gates. (Prov. 31:10-12, 25-31)

The works of a good woman, like those of a good man, speak for her, and the remarkable accomplishments of the Mormon women who gave all for the gospel of Christ certainly speak for the strength, virtue, faith, and loveliness of those heroic women. "Never till now [this last dispensation] did woman essay such an extraordinary character; never before did woman rise to the conception of so supreme a mission in her own person and life."[4]

Women Who Were First

Near the completion of the Kirtland Temple, the Prophet Joseph entered the sacred edifice to find a number of the sisters hanging curtains they had made to divide the main assembly room into four compartments for classes. As the Prophet observed the industry of the sisters, he praised them and blessed them: "The sisters are always the first in all good endeavors. Mary was the first at the tomb the morning of the resurrection, and now the sisters of the Church are the first to beautify the temple."[5]

Women were the first in many great events in Church history. Mother Lucy Mack Smith was the first to hear and believe her prophet-son's story of the glorious vision in the Sacred Grove. Rhoda Young Greene, the wife of John P. Greene, was the first to read a copy of the Book of Mormon left with her minister-husband. She encouraged him to read it, then took it to her brother, Brigham Young, who read it. She also encouraged several others to read it; and because of her, some of the greatest leaders ever to come into the Church were converted.

Jennetta Richards, a girl in her teens, was the first person confirmed a member of the Church in England. After Heber C. Kimball had baptized and confirmed her a member of the Church, he met young Willard Richards, an unmarried doctor from Boston, who had joined the Church and had accompanied Elder Kimball and the first missionaries to England. His first words to Dr. Richards were: "Willard, I baptized your wife today." Willard and Jennetta had not yet met each other. The time was March, 1838. Some months later, following the meeting of this young couple, the young doctor missionary walked with her and another young lady through the park one day. While walking with these two sisters, Willard remarked: "Richards is a good name; I never want to change it; do you, Jennetta?"

"No, I do not," was her reply, "and I think I never will." And she didn't, for she became the wife of Willard, 29 September 1839.[6]

The first child born in The Church of Jesus Christ of Latter-day Saints in Great Britain was the daughter of James and Nancy Smithies. After her birth, the parents wanted to take her to the Church of England and have her "christened," or "sprinkled," as they called it. Elder Kimball used his power of persuasion to try to induce them against such folly. They answered, "If she dies, she cannot have a burial in the churchyard." Elder Heber C. Kimball, filled with the power of God, looked at them and said: "Brother and Sister Smithies, I say unto you, in the name of Israel's God, she shall not die on this land, for she shall live until she becomes a mother in Israel, and I say it in the name of Jesus Christ and by virtue of the Holy Priesthood vested in me." That silenced them.

Mary Smithies did live. She grew to womanhood. She emigrated with her parents to America and became Heber's wife and the mother of five of his children.[7]

Lucy Clayton Bullock, the wife of Thomas Bullock, was the first of the Saints to enter Carthage jail after the martyrdom of Joseph the Prophet and Hyrum the Patriarch. And like Mary Magdalene before the yawning tomb, she fell down and wept. She was among the last, however, because of her husband's illness, to leave Nauvoo. She was among the sick and dying Saints huddled along the west bank of the Mississippi River, following their forced expulsion from Nauvoo, who were miraculously fed with quails, like Israel of old in the wilderness by the Red Sea.

It is noteworthy that the first Russian to join the Church was a woman, who was, incidentally, a countess. Her name was Josephine Ursenbach. She took it upon herself to seek out the genealogy of many of her aristocratic compeers of Europe and perform the beautiful ordinance of baptism in their behalf. The Empress Josephine and Napoleon's wife, Louisa of Austria, were among the number, as also was Elizabeth I, Queen of England.[8]

Rachel Ivins Grant

There once was a wonderful woman with a beautiful complexion who was asked what kind of cosmetics she used. She replied: "I use for my lips truth; for my voice, prayer; for my eyes, pity; for my hands, charity; for my figure, uprightness; for my heart, love." Such will be said of the women of Mormondom. They loved the truth and forsook all earthly things for it.

Rachel Ivins, a devout young woman, was the daughter of Dutch Quakers. One of her parents died when she was six years of age and the other when she was nine. She was reared under Quaker influence in the home of a very wealthy cousin. She grew up in luxury and comfort. And although she was not required to do housework, she became very skillful in the arts of homemaking. "She layeth her hands to the spindle, and her hands hold the distaff." (Proverbs 31:19.)

At the age of sixteen, this young woman joined the Baptist Church with full consent of her relatives. A short time after her affiliation with the Baptist faith, she went to Hornerstown, New Jersey, to visit an uncle. While at his home, she heard of a meeting where Mormon missionaries were preaching, so she went to hear their message. Shortly after attending this "Mormon meeting," she met the minister of the Baptist Church in which she had a pew. He had heard of her going to hear the despised Mormons and was very angry over her "infidelity."

"Miss Ivins," he said, "you went to hear those awful Mormons. If you go to hear them again your pew in my church will be vacant."

It has been said, and rightly too, that a Dutchman is the most stubborn creature on earth; and when the minister threatened to take away her pew if she went to hear the "awful Mormons" again, this young lady's "Dutch" was aroused and she replied: "My pew is vacant in your church. I shall go to hear those Mormons, and I shall pray. It may be that they have the truth."

She had not attended her first Latter-day Saint meeting with a prayerful heart, however. She had gone merely to please her sister and a girlfriend. In fact, she had felt so ashamed after having attended the meeting that upon her return home she had knelt down by her bed and asked the Lord to forgive her for doing such a wicked thing as listening to false prophets on the Sabbath day.

But now, the narrowness of her minister stirred within her the determination to continue to hear the message of the Mormon missionaries. She not only listened to their message but also prayed about it, and she was converted. The men who were instrumental in her conversion were the Prophet Joseph Smith and Erastus Snow.

Rachel's brothers were greatly disturbed over her joining the Mormon Church. Being very well-to-do financially, they offered to settle an annuity on her for life if she would only renounce her religion. One of her brothers said to her, "Rachel, you have disgraced the name of Ivins. We never want to see you again if you stay with those awful Mormons . . . but come back in a year; come back in five years, come back in ten or twenty years, and no matter when you come back, the latch string will be out, and affluence and ease will be your portion."

But this brave girl would rather cast her lot with a people who loved God and served him, even in poverty, than exchange this newly acquired "Pearl of Great Price" for all of mammon's glitter. She journeyed to Utah with her fellow exiles, married a young man who was a counselor to President Brigham Young, and became the mother of a boy who became President of the Church. Her husband died when that baby was only nine days old, and she was left in dire poverty. If she had not had burning in her bosom the testimony that Joseph Smith was a prophet of God and that the gospel was true, all she needed to do was return to her wealthy brothers who would gladly have taken care of her.

Was all this sacrifice for the truth worthwhile? Yes, many times over! Her prophet-son Heber J. Grant, after her death, praised his mother thus: "I owe everything to my mother; the marvelous teachings, the faith, the integrity of my mother have been an inspiration to me."[9] In very deed, "Her children arise up, and call her blessed." (Proverbs 31:28.)

Amanda Barnes Smith

The heroines of the Church used for their voices prayer. Prayer is the soul of religion; it is power; it gives strength to the weak, comfort to the sorrowful, courage to the timid. There were times in the early days of this Church when prayer to God was the only source of help the Saints had. Stripped of all earthly possessions, driven from their homes, prayer was their only shelter in the icy cold of winter. With loved ones in prison, or in flight from the ruthless enemy, or even killed by the barbarous hordes of Satan's legions, women were left alone—alone, and yet not alone, for their God did uphold them. "I will not forsake thee," he had promised, and they believed him.

Sister Amanda Smith suffered through the awful Haun's Mill massacre where she lost her husband and little son who were brutally killed by a mob more fiendish than human. Another of her sons—a boy named Alma—had his hip shot away by the inhuman butchers, who considered killing a pleasing sport if Mormons were the game. This heroine of Mormonism carried her wounded boy to a house some distance from the scene of the massacre and dressed his hip.

"Alma, my child," she said, "you believe that the Lord made your hip?"

"Yes, Mother."

"Well, the Lord can make something there in the place of your hip; don't you believe he can, Alma?"

"Do you think that the Lord can, Mother?" inquired the boy in his childish simplicity.

"Yes, my son," replied his heroic mother. "He has shown it all to me in a vision!"

Then she laid him comfortably, face downward, and told him not to move and the Lord would make a new hip for him.

For five weeks the boy lay in this position, and then he was entirely recovered. A flexible gristle grew over the place of the missing joint and socket, which remained a marvel to all and especially to the physicians.

One day as Sister Amanda was returning to the house with a bucket of water she heard the screams of the children. Running to the house in fright, she saw her son Alma dancing about, and the children were screaming in astonishment and joy.

Almost all the families of the Saints had fled out of Missouri except for a few families of the bereaved widows who had gathered at the house of David Evans, two miles from the scene of the massacre. In this utter desolation, what could these poor women do but pray? And pray they did. Prayer was their only source of comfort; their Heavenly Father was their only help, for none but he could deliver them.

One day a mobber came to the house with the captain's fiat: "The captain says that if you women don't stop your d— praying he will send down a posse and kill every d— one of you!"

And although prayer was their only source of strength they must live for their families' sake, and their prayers were hushed in terror. These helpless sisters dared not lift their voices to be heard in supplication. They could pray in bed or in silence, but a sorrowing, desolate heart must give vocal utterance or die. "This godless silence was more intolerable than had been the night of the massacre."[10]

Sister Amanda Smith could bear it no longer. She must hear her own voice in petition to her Heavenly Father. When the opportunity afforded itself she stole away, down into a cornfield, and crawled into a shock of corn. To her it was a temple of the Lord, a sanctuary where she could commune with her God. She prayed aloud and most fervently. She poured out her soul—anguished and sorrowful—to the Almighty Healer. As she emerged from the corn, a voice as plain as any she had ever heard spoke, repeating to her a verse of one of our great hymns:

> The soul that on Jesus hath leaned for repose
> I will not, I cannot, desert to his foes;
> That soul, though all hell should endeavor to
>   shake,
> I'll never, no never, no never forsake.

—"How Firm a Foundation," no. 85

From that moment on she had no more fear and the strength and courage received from that prayer opened the way, even at the hands of the ones who had butchered her loved ones, for her to leave Missouri in safety.[11]

> There is a bridge, whereof the span
> Is rooted in the heart of man,
> And reaches, without pile or rod,
> Unto the Great White Throne of God.
> Its traffic is in human sighs
> Fervently wafted to the skies,
> 'Tis the one pathway from despair;
> And it is called the Bridge of Prayer.

—Gilbert Thomas

Heroic Marys

In the rise of the Church of Christ out of the wilderness in these last days, there were heroic women named Mary, who were among the most loyal, devoted, and persevering disciples of the latter-day kingdom of God. They were faithful to the cause of Christ, never wavering in their trust in God's divinely appointed Prophet Joseph Smith. They, like the early Christian Marys, were witnesses of the things of God and active participants in the rise of the Church. The first of these Marys was Mary Whitmer, mother of witnesses to the Book of Mormon and of charter members of the Church. She was the first and only woman to see the gold plates from which the Prophet Joseph translated the Book of Mormon.

One morning after Joseph Smith, his wife Emma, and Oliver Cowdery came to live with the Whitmers in Fayette, New York, to complete the translation of that Nephite record, Mary Whitmer was going out to the shed to milk the cows. She was met by Moroni, the angel who delivered the plates to the Prophet, who said to her: "You have been very faithful and diligent in your labors, but you are tired because of the increase of your toil; it is proper therefore that you should have a witness that your faith might be strengthened." The angel then showed her the plates. He turned the leaves one by one. They were held together with three rings.

David Whitmer, her son, reported: "My father and mother had a large family of their own; the addition to it of Joseph, his wife Emma, and Oliver, very greatly increased the toil and anxiety of my mother. And although she never complained, she had sometimes felt that her labor was too much. This circumstance, however, completely removed all such feelings and nerved her up for her increased responsibilities."[12]

And then there were these other women of integrity named Mary: Mary Fielding, wife of the martyr Hyrum and mother of prophets; Mary Bailey, wife of Samuel, the brother of the prophet; Mary Ann Angel, wife of the prophet Brigham Young; and Mary Elizabeth Rollins, a devotee and witness of the presence of Christ. She was the first member of the Church to read the Book of Mormon in Kirtland, Ohio.

When Mary Elizabeth was ten years of age, she and her mother Keziah Ketural Rollins moved to Kirtland, Ohio, and lived with her uncle Algernon Sidney Gilbert, who was married to Keziah's sister Elizabeth Rollins. John D. Rollins, Mary Elizabeth's father, was shipwrecked on Lake Ontario during a terrible storm, and was drowned. His body was not recovered.

Shortly after their arrival in Kirtland, Oliver Cowdery, Parley P. Pratt, Peter Whitmer, Jr., and Ziba Peterson came to town preaching a new religion: the gospel had been restored and God had raised up a prophet who had translated a volume of scriptures called the Book of Mormon. Mary Elizabeth reported: "Quite a number of the residents of Kirtland were baptized, among them Mother and myself. This was the month of October 1830."[13]

A few weeks after Oliver Cowdery and his fellow missionaries left for Missouri, John Whitmer arrived from Fayette, New York, with copies of the Book of Mormon. Mary Elizabeth learned that Isaac Morley, the president of the Kirtland Branch, who owned a large farm, had a copy of that book, so she walked over to the Morley home and asked him to let her borrow his copy of the Book of Mormon. Morley was startled and surprised, "My child, I have not read one chapter of it myself, and the brethren will want to see it tonight at the meeting." But Mary Elizabeth, with tears welling in her eyes pleaded for the book. "Well," said Brother Morley, "if you will bring this book back to me before breakfast tomorrow morning, you may take it, but mind you are careful that no harm may come of it."

Mary Elizabeth happily ran to Uncle Gilbert's home

clutching the Book of Mormon to her breast. Entering the door she excitedly uttered, "Uncle, I have the Gold Bible." Consternation was felt by all in the house and she was reprimanded for being so presumptuous as to ask Brother Morley for the book before he read it. But that evening they all took turns reading the Nephite scriptures until a very late hour.

Before daylight Mary Elizabeth was up and memorized the first paragraph of First Nephi by heart. This would be the equivalent of the first five verses in our present editions of the Book of Mormon. She then sped over to the Morley house and found Brother Morley scraping the ashes from the kitchen stove. Very much surprised, he exclaimed, "Well, you are early. I guess you did not read much of it." With proud delight Mary Elizabeth showed him she had read the two books of Nephi. He was even more surprised but doubted if she could tell him what she had read. She reviewed for him an outline of the history of Nephi and quoted the first paragraph. Amazed he said, "Child, you take this book back and finish reading it. I can wait."

Before she completed her reading of the Book of Mormon the Prophet Joseph Smith arrived in Kirtland and moved into the upper rooms of the Gilbert and Whitney store. One day Newel K. Whitney brought the Prophet over to the Gilbert home on some business connected with the store. The Prophet noticed the Book of Mormon on the shelf and inquired how it got there. Sidney Gilbert told him how his niece had been so bold as to borrow it from Brother Morley. Joseph the Prophet then asked, "Where is your niece?" Mary Elizabeth was outside the house in the back yard at the time. She was called into the house. The Prophet looked at her so earnestly that she felt he could read her every thought. He made her a present of the Book of Mormon. "I will give Brother Morley another copy," he said.

A few evenings after this visit to the Gilbert home,

Mary Elizabeth and her mother walked over to where the Prophet Joseph and his wife, Emma, resided. They wanted to hear more about the Book of Mormon. There were many other visitors gathered. When the Prophet saw his guests, he said, "We might as well have a meeting." Mary Elizabeth and her mother were sitting on a plank resting on two boxes.

After prayer and singing, the Prophet Joseph began to address his guests. Suddenly he stopped and seemed almost transfixed. He looked beyond his audience. His countenance changed and he stood mute. His face turned a luminous white and seemed transparent. It appeared as though he had a search light within him. His face outshone the candle which was on the shelf just behind him. Mary Elizabeth thought she could almost see his cheek bones. He then looked at his audience very solemnly and asked, "Brothers and Sisters, do you know who has been in your midst this night?" One of the Smith family said, "An angel of the Lord." Joseph made no reply. Martin Harris, sitting on a box near the Prophet, slid to his knees, clapped Joseph around his knees and solemnly said, "I know, it was our Lord and Savior Jesus Christ."

The Prophet placed his hand on Harris' head and answered, "Martin, God revealed that to you." Then to the rest in the room: "Brothers and Sisters, the Savior has been in your midst. I want you to remember it. He cast a veil over your eyes for you could not endure to look upon Him. I want you to remember this as if it were the last thing that escaped my lips."

He knelt down and prayed. Mary Elizabeth said she had never heard such a soul-depth prayer. She felt he was talking to the Lord and spiritual power rested upon the entire congregation. This is the only meeting of its kind recorded and we are indebted to Mary Elizabeth Rollins for preserving it for us.

As a teenager, while living with the Saints in Jackson County, Missouri, called Zion, Mary Elizabeth was given the gift of tongues and the interpretation of tongues. The gift of tongues was widespread among the Church members in Zion. When Mary Elizabeth heard Oliver Cowdery, John Whitmer, and Thomas B. Marsh speak in tongues while addressing the Saints on the Sabbath day, she wanted to understand what they were saying. She prayed to the Lord to give her the meaning of their words. Once Oliver Cowdery gave a sermon in tongues. Mary Elizabeth, then fourteen years of age, interpreted. According to her interpretation, he said the Saints were going to be driven from Zion. This disturbed the Church members very much. Some wrote the Prophet Joseph, then residing in Kirtland, saying that Mary Elizabeth was talking with an evil spirit, but the Prophet's reply was, "What she has said is true."

When the mob in Jackson County started molesting the Saints, some of the mobsters rushed upon William W. Phelps' home wherein the printing press was located. They tore down the press on which Phelps had printed three thousand copies of *The Book of Commandments,* threw it out of doors, pied the type, and carried the copies out of the building, throwing them in a pile in the yard to burn. Mary Elizabeth and her sister Caroline, hiding behind the rail fence, tremblingly watched the men throw the copies of the book onto the pile and heard them scornfully utter, "Here are the Mormon commandments. We'll burn them up!"

Mary Elizabeth was determined to save some of the copies from being burned. Her sister Caroline said, "I'll go with you, but they will kill us." While the rioters' backs were turned, prying out the gable end of the house, the two teenage girls ran to the pile. They grabbed their arms full of the scriptures, tucked them in their long aprons, and fled. Some of the mob saw them and yelled, "Stop, you little wenches!" Two of the mobocrats sped after them. The girls slipped through a gap in the fence and ran into a large cornfield where they fell breathless.

Between the rows of heavy corn they laid the copies of the revelations on the ground and spread themselves securely over them. The two men searched among the tall stalks, coming very near the girls whose hearts beat frantically. Finally the searchers gave up and left. Joining the other men, they completely razed the Phelps's home to the ground.

The copies of the Lord's commandments snatched by the Rollins sisters were bound and given to the leading brethren of the Church. One bound copy was sent to Mary Elizabeth which she "prized very highly."[14]

Sarah Melissa Granger Kimball

Sarah M. Kimball had the idea and carried out the organization of the sisters in her neighborhood into a society to make clothes for the workmen on the Nauvoo Temple. She desired to do all in her power and strength to assist in the building of the Nauvoo Temple.

When Sarah's eldest son was three days old, the Prophet Joseph Smith was in need of money to raise the walls of the temple. She wished to help, but was timid about asking her husband, Hiram, who was a wealthy man but not then a member of the Church, to contribute for her sake.

Her husband came to her bedside, and as he was admiring their three-day-old son, Sarah asked: "What is the boy worth?"

Hiram replied: "Oh, I don't know. He is worth a great deal."

Sarah pressed, "Is he worth a thousand dollars?"

"Yes, more than that if he lives and does well."

Sarah said, "Half of him is mine, is it not?"

"Yes, I suppose so," agreed her husband.

"Then I have something to help on the temple."

Hiram answered pleasantly, "You have?"

"Yes, and I'm thinking of turning my share in as tithing."

"Well, I'll think about that," said Hiram.

Soon afterwards Hiram Kimball met the Prophet Joseph Smith and said to him, "Sarah has got the advantage of me this time. She proposed to turn out the boy as Church property."

The Prophet was pleased with the joke and told Mr. Kimball, "I accept all such donations and from this day the boy shall stand recorded, Church property." Then turning to Willard Richards, his secretary, he instructed: "Make a record of this, and you are my witness." The Prophet then addressed Hiram Kimball: "Major, (he was a major in the Nauvoo Legion) you now have the privilege of paying $500 and retaining possession, or receiving $500 and giving possession."

Hiram asked Joseph if city property was good currency.

"Yes, indeed," replied the Prophet.

"How will that city lot north of the temple suit you?"

And Joseph nodding, replied, "It is just what we want."

After Sarah got up and around, the Prophet Joseph met her one day and said, "You have consecrated your firstborn son. For this you are blessed of the Lord. I bless you in the name of the Lord God of Abraham, Isaac, and Jacob. And I seal upon you all the blessings that pertain to the faithful."[15]

Jane Grover

One of the really great stories of feminine heroism occurred near Council Bluffs while the Saints were camped there enroute to the Rocky Mountains. Seventeen-year-old Jane Grover, on a beautiful summer morning, went with two other sisters in a wagon with Patriarch Nathan Tanner and his little granddaughter to gather gooseberries. When they reached the woods, the old gentleman rested while they picked the berries.

While gathering berries, Jane and the little grand-daughter had strayed some distance from the rest when suddenly they heard shouts. The little girl thought it was her grandfather shouting and was about to answer when Jane restrained her. Jane was sure the shouting came from Indians. They hurried toward the wagon and upon coming in sight of it they saw Father Tanner running his team around and around. Jane thought this was very strange, but as she approached nearer she saw Indians gathering around the wagon, whooping and yelling as others joined them.

Jane and the little granddaughter leaped into the wagon with Father Tanner. He made an effort to start his team away from the Indians hoping to drive speedi-ly to the Mormon encampment when four Indians grabbed the wagon wheels and two others seized the horses by the bits. The fifth big redskin climbed into the wagon to take Jane. She was very frightened and tried to jump out the opposite side and run for help. Father Tanner restrained her, "No, my poor child; it is too late!" Jane told him the Indians should not take her alive. The old gentleman's face was as white as a sheet, for by now the Indians were stripping him. They had taken his watch, his handkerchief, and knife, and at the same time were trying to pull him from the wagon.

Jane began to pray silently to her Heavenly Father. While she prayed and struggled against the Indian, who now had hold of her, the Spirit of the Almighty fell upon her. She was given to know the Indians' inten-tions to kill Father Tanner, burn the wagon, and take the women captive. She freed herself from the grasp of the red man and stood upon her feet with great power. No tongue can describe her feelings. She was as happy as a Saint could be when but a few moments before she saw worse than death staring her in the face. She was now filled with the power of God and she spoke to the

Indians in their own language.

Upon hearing Jane's first words the sons of Laman let go their hold upon the horses and upon the wagon wheels. The little girl and Father Tanner looked on in speechless astonishment. The Indians stood in front of Jane while she talked to them by the power of God. They bowed before her and answered, "Yes," and Jane understood.

The Lord gave her part of the interpretation of her own words, and she said to the red marauders:

> I suppose you Indian warriors think you are going to kill us? Don't you know the Great Spirit is watching you and knows everything in your hearts? We have come out here to gather some of our Father's fruit. We have not come to injure you; and if you harm us the Great Spirit shall smite you to the earth. We are the Lord's people and so are you; but you must cease your murders and wickedness; the Lord is displeased with it and will not prosper you if you continue in it. You think you own this land, this timber, this water, all the horses. Why, you do not own one thing on earth, not even the air you breathe—it belongs to the Great Spirit.[16]

When she stopped speaking, the Indians shook hands with her, Father Tanner, and the little girl. They returned all that they had taken from him and received in return some crackers and berries from Jane. Jane, like Queen Esther of old, had saved her friends.

Sarah Pea Rich

> . . . Intreat me not to leave thee, or to return from following after thee: for whither thou goest, I will go; and where thou lodgest, I will lodge: thy people shall be my people, and thy God my God:
>
> Where thou diest, I will die, and there will I be buried: the Lord do so to me, and more also, if ought but death part thee and me. (Ruth 1:16-17.)

These immortal words of Ruth, the Moabitess, have echoed through the ages as the most perfect expression of love and duty ever uttered and have found root and new growth and warmth in the bosoms of the heroic women of the Church.

Sarah Pea of Looking-Glass Prairie, Illinois, was a beautiful girl, one of three daughters of John and Elizabeth Pea. They belonged to the Reformed Methodist Church until two Mormon elders came to their home in the summer of 1835. Meetings were held in the Pea home, the gospel preached, and the Book of Mormon read. On a Friday night, six weeks after the elders had left Looking-Glass Prairie for Ohio, Sarah dreamed prophetically that the elders would come to her parents' house the next evening. Saturday morning her father and mother went to Belleville. At the breakfast table, she asked her father if he would not try to be home early.

The father asked, "Why are you so particular? Is your young man coming?"

Sarah replied, "No, but those two Mormon elders will be here tonight."

Her father inquired if she had heard from them.

"No," came Sarah's answer, "but I dreamed last night that they would be here, and I feel sure it will be so."

Father Pea laughed and told Sarah she must be crazy, for those Mormons were hundreds of miles away.

After they had driven away, Sarah encouraged her sister to help clean house in preparation for the coming elders. Her sister laughed at Sarah, but helped with the baking and other preparations for Sunday.

And, sure enough, as the sun was sinking, the two elders made their appearance—walking up the lane just as Sarah had seen them in her dream. Sarah met them on the porch with a welcome which startled them, "I have been looking for you to come."

They inquired how she knew; and after she had told

them of her dream, the elders said, "Well, we had a dream that we were to return here and baptize you and build up the Church in the region."

Sarah and her family continued to investigate the restored gospel, and on 15 December 1835, Sarah was initiated into the Kingdom of God even though the elders had to cut the ice that she might be baptized. Following her conversion, the missionaries expressed grave concern lest she should fall in love with an outsider and marry one not of the faith. They cautioned her unmarried sister as well. One of the elders said to Sarah one day, "I have taken the liberty of recommending you to a very fine young man, who I believe would make you a good companion."

A few months later, another missionary, while talking to the family about gathering to Missouri, said to Sarah, "I have a good young elder picked out for you." To the surprise of all, the young elder he named proved to be the same one that the former elder had so highly recommended to her. This caused no end of teasing and bantering at Sarah's expense.

A few weeks later the elders who had baptized the family returned for a visit; and one of them said to Sarah, "While I was in Kirtland, I recommended you to a very worthy young man, who is an elder in the Church; and when I told him of you, he said, 'That same girl has been recommended to me twice before, and now I must hunt her up.'"

Sarah was very much astonished when, on inquiring his name, she heard the same name which had been twice before recommended to her. She made this comment: "We all wondered, thinking how strange this should be!"

About a month after this last conversation, Sarah received a letter, postmarked St. Louis, Missouri. Imagine her surprise when she read:

Miss Sarah Pea:

It is with pleasure that I at this time pen a few lines to you, although a perfect stranger to you. However, I trust that these few lines may be received by you, and may be the beginning of a happy acquaintance with you.

I will now let you know the reason for my boldness in writing to you. It is because Elder G. M. Hinkle and others have highly recommended you as a saint of the last days, as being worthy of my attention.

I think I should be happy to get a good companion, such a one as I could take comfort with through life, and such a one as could take comfort with me. As you have been recommended to me as such, I should be very happy to see you and converse with you on the subject. . . .

Yours with the best of respects,
Charles C. Rich

After reading this extraordinary message, Sarah pondered deeply upon her answer. She began thinking more seriously of marriage. What should she do about it? She prayed over the problem, for she firmly believed that the hand of the Lord was in it. She had always prayed that she might be led by the Spirit of the Lord in the selection of a companion for life; and now, as never before, she wanted him to guide her. The next step Sarah took was to go to the Bible, for help. She had been reared a Methodist; so, as John Wesley was wont to do whenever he was perplexed, she took down the family Bible, closed her eyes, flipped open the pages at random, and placed her finger upon a verse—Ruth 1:16-17. Opening her eyes, she read the words under her finger. There, sure enough, was her answer, as plain as the words before her. She immediately took paper, pen, and ink and wrote her answer:

Mr. Charles C. Rich:

Intreat me not to leave thee, or to return from following after thee; for whither thou goest, I will go; and where thou lodgest, I will lodge: thy people shall be my people, and thy God my God: Where thou diest, I will die, and there will be buried: the Lord do so to me, and more also, if aught but death part thee and me.

With great respect, I remain
Yours truly,
Sarah Pea

Six and a half months transpired before Sarah met Charles, but they met and were not disappointed. Four months after their meeting they were married by the first of the match-makers—George M. Hinkle.[17]

Sarah also became the agent for an inspired healing. Women's exercise of spiritual gifts was fully in accordance with the gospel equality taught by the Prophet Joseph Smith. The rewards such as the gift of the Holy Ghost and temple ordinances, are alike for men and women. The doctrine of equal rights is confirmed in the ordinances of the Church, which are alike for men and women. The man who holds the priesthood officiates in it, but the blessings of it descends upon the woman also.[18]

Joseph Smith taught this equality. A complaint came to him that women had administered "to the sick by the power of faith, the laying on of hands and anointing with oil." His answer was:

Who are better qualified to administer than our faithful and zealous sisters, whose hearts are full of faith, tenderness, sympathy, and compassion? No one. I gave a lecture on the priesthood, showing how the sisters could come in possession of the privileges, blessings, and gifts of the priesthood, and that the signs should follow them, such as healing the sick, casting out devils, etc. And that they might attain unto these blessings by virtuous life and conversation, and diligence in keeping all the commandments.[19]

Many sisters in our history exercised this right and the sick were healed. While crossing the plains of Iowa, the Riches had with them a young man named George

Patten. He had been left motherless when he was seven years old. After being baptized into the Church, he was taken into the Rich household and was cared for as though he were a son. As our story opens he is eighteen years of age.

About ninety miles east of Garden Grove, one of the temporary settlements of the Saints, Patten became very ill. He lay in the rocking wagon for three weeks. When they arrived at Garden Grove his hip bones showed clearly through the skin. Many thought he would surely die, but President Young blessed him that he should live. Charles and Sarah took very good care of him and did all they could to save him. He was put to bed in a tent, but it looked as though he would die at any moment. One night Sarah relieved her husband, who had been sitting at the bedside of the boy, so that he could snatch a few minutes sleep.

She looked down upon the boy more dead than alive stretched out on the couch and pondered, "What would I do, if he were my own flesh and blood?" Then she knelt down and prayed—prayed that the Lord would show her what to do for the restoration of the boy.

When she arose from her knees, she felt impressed to put a teaspoonful of consecrated oil in his mouth. The lad's tongue was drawn far back in his mouth and was very black, and his eyes appeared to be set in his head. She afterward anointed his face and head with oil, and as she did so asked the Lord to bless him. In a few moments she gave him another teaspoonful of oil, and to her great joy she observed that he swallowed it. She later gave him some liquid nourishment which he also swallowed. Then she washed his hands and face in water and soda. All night long Sarah worked over George Patten and at daybreak, to her joy and satisfaction, he opened his eyes and looked at her with sheer astonishment. Joyously Sarah asked: "George, do you know me?" And he answered in a whisper, "Yes!"

What merciful, tender angels these marvelous women of the Church are! Their importance and influence cannot be over-estimated nor over-esteemed. President Brigham Young once said:

> Now, a few words to my sisters here in the Kingdom of God. We want your influence and power in helping to build that Kingdom and what I wish to say to you is simply this: if you will govern and control yourselves in all things in accordance with good, sound common sense and the principles of truth and righteousness, there is not the least fear but what father, uncle, grandfather, brothers, and sons will follow in your wake.[20]

For one, I am more than willing to follow in the wake of these great women, molders of human destiny; embodiment of faith, devotion, tenderness, compassion, love, humility, and loyalty—such a perfect host of magnificent womanhood. Their story of faith is so strange, so thrilling, "so rare in its elements of experience, that neither history nor fable affords a perfect example."[21]

All hail to the heroines of the Church, for their own works indeed praise them in the gates!

Notes

[1] Edward W. Tullidge, *The Women of Mormondom* (New York City: Tullidge and Crandall, 1877), p. 1.

[2] N. B. Lundwall (compiler and publisher), *The Vision* (Salt Lake City, Utah, 1942), pp. 145-148.

[3] Tullidge, op cit, p. 3.

[4] Tullidge, p. 1.

[5] *Ibid.*, p. 76.

[6] Orson F. Whitney, *Life of Heber C. Kimball* (Salt Lake City, Utah: Stevens & Wallis, Inc. 1945), pp. 143-44.

[7] Whitney, pp. 156-57.

8 Tullidge, p. 474.

9 Heber J. Grant, *Gospel Standards* (Salt Lake City, Utah: Deseret News Press, 1941), pp. 351-52.

10 Tullidge, p. 129.

11 Tullidge, pp. 128-32.

12 L.D.S. Messenger and Advocate, Kirtland, Ohio, 1834-1837, April 1835, p. 112.

13 Mary Elizabeth Rollins Lightner, "Diary of Mary Elizabeth Rollings Lightner," copied by Brigham Young University Library, 1960, p. 1.

14 Lightner, p. 10.

15 Women's Exponent, xii (September 1, 1883), p. 51.

16 Tullidge, pp. 474-477.

17 Leonard J. Arrington, *Charles C. Rich, Mormon General and Western Frontiersman* (Provo, Utah: Brigham Young University Press, 1974), p. 57.

18 John A. Widtsoe, *Joseph Smith—Seeker After Truth* (Salt Lake City, Utah: Deseret News Press, 1951), pp. 185-88.

19 Joseph Fielding Smith, *Teachings of the Prophet Joseph Smith* (Salt Lake City, Utah: Deseret Book, 1970), pp. 229, 231.

20 John A. Widtsoe, ed., *Discourses of Brigham Young* (Salt Lake City, Utah: Deseret Book 1925), p. 309.

21 Tullidge, p. 1.

Lucy Mack Smith:
Mother in Israel

Lucy Mack Smith was foremost an inspirational influence in the life of her prophet-son. On 18 December 1833, he praised and blessed his mother in these words:

> And blessed is my mother, for she is a mother in Israel, and shall be a partaker with my father in all his patriarchal blessings. . . . Blessed is my mother for her soul is ever filled with benevolence and philanthropy, and notwithstanding her age, she shall yet receive strength and be comforted in the midst of her house, and thus saith the Lord, she shall have eternal life.[1]

Again in 1842, when the Prophet Joseph was recording his feelings toward his brethren and his family, he wrote: "My mother also is one of the noblest and best of all women. May God grant to prolong her days and mine, that we may live to enjoy each other's society long, yet in the enjoyment of liberty, and to breathe the free air."[2]

On the July 8, 1775, four days after the signing of the Declaration of Independence and on the day when this immortal document was read to the public in

Philadelphia, Pennsylvania, Lucy Mack was born to Solomon Mack and Lydia Gates Mack, in the little town of Gilsum, Cheshire County, New Hampshire. Lucy was the youngest of a family of eight children. The oldest of Lucy Mack Smith's descendants today are of the sixth generation from this noble grandmother.

Lucy's father was a veteran of the French and Indian War and of the War for Independence. He was a loyal patriot and a devout believer in the Supreme Ruler of the Universe. He was also a kind, sympathetic father, ever interested in the progress and success of his children. But it was from her mother, Lydia Gates Mack, that Lucy received her training, her sterling faith in God, courage, determination, trust in the providence of the Almighty, and belief in the Bible as the word of God. All these were bequeathed to Lucy by a faithful mother. Lucy's mother was a talented woman and her husband, Solomon, was ever ready to recognize those talents and praise his wife for them.

After moving to Marlow, New Hampshire, which was a sparsely populated area, Lydia Mack trained her family in the rudiments of learning. Solomon recorded:

> Here I was thrown into a situation to appreciate more fully the talents and virtues of my excellent wife; for as our children were deprived of schools, she assumed the charge of their education, and performed the duties of an instructress as none, save a mother, is capable of. Precepts accompanied by examples such as hers were calculated to make impressions on the minds of the young, never to be forgotten.[3]

When Lucy was eight, her mother became dangerously ill. During her sickness, she called her family to her bedside and counseled her children to remember the instructions she had given them "to fear God and to walk uprightly before him." Fearing that her mortal probation was near its end, she requested Stephen, her second son, to take care of Lucy, her baby. This he promised to do, but the mother recovered and lived to within a few months of the time of her grandson, Joseph's first vision.

At the age of nineteen, while Lucy was visiting her brother, Stephen, in Tunbridge, Vermont, she met a young man named Joseph Smith. He was tall, athletically built, good-looking, inoffensive but aggressive. At the time of their meeting, he was doing very well as a farmer. After a brief courtship they were married, 24 January 1796, at Tunbridge.

Few couples today receive a thousand-dollar wedding present, but Lucy did. When it was known in Tunbridge that she was to become a bride, John Mudget, the business partner of her brother Stephen, said, "Lucy ought to have something worth naming, and I will give her just as much as you will."

"Done," responded Stephen, "I will give her five hundred dollars in cash."

"Good," said John, "and I will give her five hundred dollars more."[4]

Lucy did not need to use that thousand dollars to help her young husband get started. No, indeed. He had a farm in Tunbridge, and was also a school teacher, and then he and his bride moved to Randolph where he opened a mercantile establishment. Yes, Lucy and her young husband began married life rather prosperously. They were both frugal, hard workers and possessed the will to succeed. And succeed they did, until an unscrupulous individual cheated them out of their investments. It was then that Lucy brought forth her thousand-dollar wedding present to save the good name of her husband and help pay off his indebtedness.

While the Smiths were living at Randolph Lucy was stricken with an illness which almost claimed her life. The doctor had given her up, and even her husband despaired of her ever recovering. But Lucy prayed all one night to the Lord, solemnly covenanting with him that if he would spare her life, she would serve him to the best of her abilities. In answer to her prayer a voice spoke to her these comforting words: "Seek and ye shall find, knock and it shall be opened unto you. Let your heart be comforted; ye believe in God, believe also in me."

Not long afterward her mother entered the room. She was overjoyed at Lucy's improvement. "Why Lucy, my dear, you are better," she joyously exclaimed. "Yes, Mother," replied Lucy, "the Lord will let me live, if I am faithful to the promise which I made to him to be a comfort to my mother, my husband, and my children."[5]

To this promise Lucy was ever true. Suffering abuse, poverty, sorrow; through pain, sickness, and death; yet she was true to her pledged word.

She became the mother of eleven children. One died in infancy, and five of her sons preceded her in death, four of the five dying while she was living in Nauvoo. Lucy Smith knew sorrow, knew it all too well, for her husband passed away before she was a year in Nauvoo, leaving her to endure alone the bereavement of her famous sons. And yet, she was not alone; for God, in whom she had always trusted, was at her side, comforting, strengthening.

She knew poverty. During her early married life, because of crop failures, she and her husband moved eight times before they arrived in western New York where their son, Joseph, was to receive his many glorious manifestations. In New York State the Smiths began anew in the spirit of optimism and determination. Even though Lucy tells us she arrived there with "barely two cents in cash," the father and the older boys found ready employment in the growing Erie Canal town of Palmyra. Industrious Mother Smith set up a business of painting oil cloth coverings, "and did extremely well." From her earnings, she furnished provisions for the family and began to replenish the household furniture.[6]

The Smiths were a friendly family, likable and easy to get along with; and, as Lucy has said, "The hand of friendship was extended on every side, and we blessed God with our whole heart, for his mercy which endureth forever."[7] According to William Smith, Joseph's younger brother, it was not until after Joseph received his visions that the neighbors thought of the Smiths as being other than good, hard-working, New England farmers.[8]

> Joseph Smith learned faith in God at his mother's knee; belief in the divinity of the Bible; belief that God hears and answers prayers; belief that God, who is the same yesterday, today, and forever, grants visions, dreams, and revelations to his children in every age, the same as he did in the early Christian era. From his mother, young Joseph was no doubt taught that there was no true church on the earth, for she, like many others contemporary with and before her, was anxiously looking forward to the day when God would once again reveal his word to man. As a young mother with a small growing family, Lucy once said, "I said in my heart that there was not then upon the earth the religion which I sought. I, therefore, determined to examine my Bible, and, taking Jesus and his disciples for my guide, endeavored to obtain from God that which man could neither give nor take away."[9]

While the Smiths were living in New York, Lucy became even more concerned about the subject of religion than she had previously been, although she had always been a firm believer in God and had faithfully read the Bible. She knew that one must be baptized if one is to enter the Kingdom of God, so she found a preacher who was willing to immerse her in water without requiring her to join his church. However, during "the Revival" of the early part of 1820, she became affiliated with the Presbyterians and followed that faith until the day of her son Joseph 's remarkable vision of the Father and Son which led to his founding the Church of Jesus Christ of Latter-day Saints.

After she heard from the lips of Joseph the glorious account of his vision of the Father and Son, she believed him. All her life she believed him. This belief led her from her home in New York to Ohio; out of Ohio to Missouri; from Missouri into Illinois—where she lived out her final days in the home of her daughter-in-law, Emma.

On the day that the Church was organized, Lucy Smith and her husband were baptized into The Church of Jesus Christ of Latter-day Saints; and from that day until the day of her death, Mother Smith was one of its most ardent defenders and advocates. What one biographer said of another great woman can also be said, and with emphasis, of Lucy Smith: Hers was "a life that was full of faith in God and alive with a passion for souls."[10]

She was "alive with a passion for souls." While traveling with a group of eighty Saints from New York to Ohio, she embraced every opportunity to teach the gospel and to bear testimony of the truth. As she and her fellow-Saints were leaving Buffalo, New York, one man cried out, "Is the Book of Mormon true?" And Mother Smith replied:

> That book was brought forth by the power of God and translated by the gift of the Holy Ghost; and if I could make my voice sound as loud as the trumpet of Michael the Archangel I would declare the truth from land to land, and from sea to sea, and the echo should reach to every isle, until every member of the family of Adam should be left without excuse. For I do testify that God has revealed himself to man again in these last days.[11]

Through letters and by personal visits, Mother Smith endeavored to interest members of her father's family in the Church. During the time she lived in Ohio, she visited some of her kinfolk in Pontiac, Michigan. While she was visiting with her brother Stephen's daughter, a protestant minister was introduced to Mother Smith. Upon shaking hands with her, he sneeringly said, "And you are the mother of that poor, foolish, silly boy, Joe Smith, who pretended to translate the Book of Mormon."

Lucy looked the Reverend Mr. Ruggles steadily in the eye as she made her reply, "I am, sir, the mother of Joseph Smith; but why do you apply to him such epithets as those?"

"Because," came the rejoinder, "he imagines he is going to break down all other churches with that simple 'Mormon' book."

Mother Smith asked "his Reverence" if he had ever read the book.

"Oh, no." It was beneath his notice.

Then the mother of the Prophet countered with a statement from Paul that an open-minded person should prove all things, and then bore her solemn testimony that the Book of Mormon contained the fullness of the everlasting gospel and "was written for the salvation of your soul by the gift and power of the Holy Ghost."

This was too much for Reverend Ruggles, who brushed off Mother Smith's witness with, "Pooh, nonsense—I'm not afraid of any member of my church being led away by that stuff; they have too much intelligence."

Mother Smith's reply was a shocking surprise to the pastor as well as being prophetic, "Now, Mr. Ruggles, mark my words—as true as God lives, before three years we will have more than one-third of your church; and sir, whether you believe it or not, we will take the very deacon too."[12] This inspired utterance was literally fulfilled.

Lucy was richly endowed with the gift of leadership. When the New York Saints were moving to Kirtland, Ohio, they unanimously chose her as their leader. It was well for them that she was their choice, for only through her initiative, resourcefulness, courage, and faith did they safely arrive in Ohio.

In a time of emergency, when leadership was needed while building a Kirtland meeting house, Lucy Smith came forth to lead out. Winter was coming on and the Saints had to have a shelter for study and worship. Joseph, Hyrum, and many other able leaders were in Missouri, and the building committee just was not getting the job done. Lucy told her husband she could raise funds for the building of the meeting place, and she did. She wrote a subscription paper on which she agreed to refund the money donated if the building did not go through. Within two weeks she had enough money to complete the job.

One of her greatest contributions to the building of the Kingdom in these latter days was her willingness to serve and her ability to do well whatever she undertook for the welfare of others. Inez Smith, a historian of the Reorganized Church of Jesus Christ of Latter-day Saints paid this tribute to the mother of the Prophet: "Hers was a service wherever she went. A nurse, a comforter, a counselor, wise, discreet, and sympathetic. A woman of action, sensitive to the necessity for immediate proceedings. . . . [She was] well fitted to be the mother of men destined to be leaders in a religious movement such as she saw her sons leading."[13]

During the seven years the Smiths lived in Kirtland and its vicinity, Lucy's husband was "several times torn from his wife by the enemies of the Saints and unjustly imprisoned, but she manifested on all such occasions a calm assurance that all would be well."[14]

In 1838, Mother Smith moved with her husband (then Patriarch to the Church) and her family to Far West, Missouri. She experienced the horrors and miseries which accompanied the ruthless order of Governor Lilburn Boggs, which read: "The Mormons must be treated as enemies and must be exterminated or driven from the state."[15] She was driven from her home in winter weather. She trudged through the snow and cold into friendly Quincy, Illinois. Before her ill-timed flight from the heartless mob-rule of Missouri, she saw her two eldest sons, Joseph and Hyrum, taken as prisoners and charged with murder, treason, arson, and larceny. In October 1838, the mob-militia officer ordered them shot. The grief-stricken mother pushed her way through the crowd to the canvas-covered wagon wherein were her imprisoned sons.

"I am the mother of the Prophet," she cried. "Is there not a gentleman here, who will assist me to that wagon, that I may take a last look at my children, and speak to them once before I die?"

But the stony-hearted people gathered about were deaf to this heart-rending plea. Still she made her way to the wagon and grasped the hand of her prophet-son Joseph as he silently thrust it under the tightly nailed canvas cover. Mother Smith, her heart pained, pled: "Joseph, do speak to your mother once more. I cannot bear to go until I hear your voice."

"God bless you, Mother," sobbed Joseph. No more.

Yet in all this anguish and anxiety over the safety of her sons she was comforted. She said, "I found consolation that surpassed all earthly comfort. I was filled with the Spirit of God."[16]

The Prophet loved his mother and often sought her counsel and delighted to confide in her. An incident illustrates how Joseph and others of his family confided in their mother. Following Joseph and his brother Hyrum's return from Missouri in August 1834, they visited their mother. Each held one of her hands in his as they related the story of their journey and of their stay in Missouri. Cholera had broken out in Zion's Camp. Over seventy were afflicted and many died. Joseph and Hyrum also fell victim to the disease. They prayed to God for deliverance, but the heavens seemed sealed.

Then, of a sudden, Hyrum sprang to his feet strangely refreshed, and exclaimed: "Joseph we shall return to our families. I have had an open vision, in which I saw mother kneeling under an apple tree; and she is even now asking God, in tears, to spare our lives, that she may again behold us in the flesh. The Spirit testifies that her prayers, united with ours, will be answered."

As Hyrum finished relating this incident, Joseph put his arm about his mother and said, "Oh, my mother! How often have your prayers been the means of assisting us when shadows of death encompassed us."[17]

A few weeks later, Lucy, Joseph, Sr., and their children moved to Quincy. They, like other exiled Saints, "suffered the hardships and privations which characterized the extermination from Missouri." After a brief stay in Quincy they moved to Commerce, a swampy bend in the Mississippi, also known as Galland's Bog. Even so, this bog was much more friendly than the Boggs from whom they had fled, and it soon grew into "Nauvoo the Beautiful."

There was only a brief respite from sorrow for Lucy Smith here. The first of her great sorrows was the passing of her patriarch-husband 14 September 1840. The exposure and ill-treatment in Missouri had left him easy prey to the disease of the swamps which laid low many a weakened Saint.

Shortly before his passing, as the family gathered around his bedside, he told his beloved companion:

"Mother, do you know that you are the mother of as great a family as ever lived upon the earth? The world loves its own, but it does not love us. It hates us because we are not of the world; therefore, all its malice is poured out upon my children. And I realize that although they were raised up to do the Lord's work, yet they must pass through scenes of trouble and afflictions as long as they live upon the earth; and I dread to leave them surrounded by enemies."[18]

Left a widow, Mother Smith lost herself in serving those less fortunate. Her house she filled like a hospital with the sick:

> Many of the sick owed the preservation of their lives to her motherly care, attention, and skill in nursing them, which she did without pecuniary consideration and the extent of which can only be appreciated by those who are personally acquainted with the dreadful scenes of sickness and distress, in consequence of the Missouri expulsion.[19]

When the Mansion House was built for the Prophet Joseph and his family, Mother Smith went to live with him and his "beloved Emma." She occupied a room of her own and was shown every kindness and consideration. That she might have a little income of her own, she turned her room into a small museum where she showed several curiosities for a small fee. They included articles from the South Seas, sent by Addison Pratt, then serving a mission in Polynesia, and the mummies purchased by the Church from Michael H. Chandler in 1835, which Mother Smith purchased and placed among her collections.

Josiah Quincy, historian and one-time mayor of Boston, visited Nauvoo as a young man in the spring of 1844. He wrote an interesting note about his visit to the Mansion House and of his seeing Mother Smith and the mummies. The Prophet was showing young Quincy about the Mansion. "And now come with me," he invited, "and I will show you the curiosities!" So saying he led the way to a lower room where sat a venerable and respectable-looking lady. "This is my mother, gentlemen. The curiosities we shall see belong to her. They were purchased with her own money at the cost of six thousand dollars." And then with deep feeling he added the words, "And that woman was turned out upon the prairie in the dead of night by a mob." Quincy writes further:

There were some pine presses against the wall of the room. These receptacles Smith opened and disclosed four human bodies, shrunken and black with age. "These are mummies," said the exhibitor. "I want you to look at that little runt of a fellow over there. He was a great man in his day, Why that was Pharaoh Necho, King of Egypt!" Some parchments inscribed with hieroglyphics were then offered us. They were preserved under glass and handled with great respect. "That is the writing of Abraham, the Father of the Faithful," said the Prophet. "Here we have the earliest account of the creation from which Moses composed the first book of Genesis." The parchment last referred to showed a crude drawing of a man and woman, and a serpent walking upon a pair of legs. After viewing the mummies Joseph closed the cabinet with "Gentlemen, those who see these curiosities generally pay my mother a quarter of a dollar."[20]

Through the years, Mother Smith watched with pride the remarkable achievements of her son, the prophet. Her soul rejoiced when, in 1841, he introduced to the Saints the glorious work of salvation for the dead, for now she could have the work done vicariously for her eldest son, Alvin, who departed from this life a few weeks following the appearance of the Angel Moroni to Joseph the Seer.

At the height of his noble career, the Prophet's life was snuffed out, along with that of his brother Hyrum, by a cowardly mob with painted faces. The death of her sons was Mother Smith's greatest sorrow, but she bore it courageously; and in her empty hours of bereavement her Father and God comforted her.

Dr. B. W. Richmond, a visitor in Nauvoo, was at the Mansion House at the time the bodies of Joseph and Hyrum were brought from Carthage. He tells of the depth of anguish and sorrow suffered by Mother Smith.

I passed into the next room, and the mother of Joseph and Hyrum came up to me with a gaze of wild despair; and clasping me with both hands she asked why they had shot her dear children. Her eyes were dry and her anguish seemed too deep for tears. She paced the room, turned around, went to the window, and then to the door of the room where Joseph's wife was still weeping.[21]

But in the midst of her anguish, a voice spoke comfortingly to her. "I have taken them to Myself, that they might have rest," it consoled. And as she looked down upon the lifeless bodies of her sons, they seemed to speak: "Mother, weep not for us; we have overcome the world by love; we carried to them the gospel, that their souls might be saved; they slew us for our testimony, and thus placed us beyond their power; their ascendancy is but for a moment, ours is an eternal triumph."[22]

In Nauvoo, she suffered the deaths of two other sons as well, one before the martyrdom and one afterward. Don Carlos, editor of the Times and Seasons and president of the high priests, though not yet twenty-six, died in August 1841. Samuel Harrison Smith, on 27 June 1844, rode to Carthage hoping to be with his brothers. He was met in the woods by some of the fleeing mob who just murdered his brothers. They recognized him as a brother of the martyrs and attempted to shoot him as he rode into Carthage. They raced madly in pursuit of the fleeing Samuel, yet he was successful in reaching his destination without being shot. The owner of the hotel rushed out to help him from the saddle and hurriedly concealed him within a room. Samuel remained in Carthage that night. The next day he assisted in taking the bodies of his brothers to Nauvoo. He never recovered from the violent chase from his would-be murderers, complaining after the chase of an intense pain in his side. He soon became fatally ill, passing away 30 July 1844, slightly over a month after the secret burial of his brothers (June 28). And thus Lucy's family was reduced to five—the widowed mother, William the only surviving son, and three daughters, Sophronia, Catherine, and Lucy.[23]

Before Wilford Woodruff went to preside over the British Mission in August 1844 he visited Mother Smith. He recorded in his journal the details of that visit:

> I next visited Mother Lucy Smith, the Mother of the Prophet, and of a large family of sons. This noble mother and prophetess felt sorely grieved over the loss of her children, and lamented the cruel treatment she had received at the hands of an unfeeling world. She begged a blessing at my hands. I laid my hands upon her head and by the Spirit of God pronounced upon her a blessing. This was August 24, 1844. I quote from that blessing as follows: "Let thy heart be comforted in the midst of thy sorrows for thou shalt be held forever in honorable remembrance in the congregation of the righteous. Thou shalt be remembered in thy wants during the remainder of thy days; and when thou shalt be called upon to depart, thou shalt lie down in peace having seen the salvation of thy God who has laid the everlasting foundation for the deliverance of Israel through the instrumentality of thy sons."[24]

This blessing was literally fulfilled.

President Brigham Young and the Twelve ever manifested and demonstrated sincere interest in Mother Smith and her widowed kindred. They did what they could for them, supplying their wants from the funds of the Church. From the Journal History, we read the following:

> August 2, 1845, Saturday. In the afternoon President Young rode out in the new Church carriage, with Brother Heber C. Kimball and the Bishop to look over two blocks of Emma Smith's which she had agreed to sell to the trustees for $550. They selected blocks 96-97, and then went to Mother Lucy Smith's and brought her in the carriage to choose which of the blocks she would have deeded to herself and daughters. She selected block 96 and desired the Church to

build her a house like Brother Kimball's. [His was one
of the largest and finest homes in Nauvoo.] She asked
for the carriage they rode in, a horse and a double carriage harness. They gave her the use of the carriage
during her lifetime.

On 9 July 1845, the Church authorities held a family
reunion for the Smith widows. All the widows and
about thirteen of the children were present. This
reunion was held in the Mansion House. President
Young, Heber C. Kimball, John Taylor, Bishop Whitney,
and Bishop Miller assisted in waiting upon the tables.
The band was present and performed appropriate
music. At the close of the meeting Lucy Smith spoke
with pathos and feeling.

When Brigham Young led the Saints west he left men
in Nauvoo as agents for the Church, disposing certain
properties and settling obligations. They were instructed
to assist Lucy and Emma Smith, who were in need.

On 13 November 1845 the Journal History records, "It
was decided that Mother Lucy Smith be furnished with
food, clothing, and wood for the winter by the trustees."

A very interesting document extant today is an
undated letter written in Lucy Smith's hand to Bishop
Newel K. Whitney:

> Beloved Brother:
> You have had the kindness to urge me to make
> known my wants more than once; as you wished me
> to have all I needed as to temporal comforts. Now, for
> this I do esteem you a most dutiful and affectionate
> son and with this feeling I apply to you in perfect con-
> fidence at this time that you may, if you can
> conveniently do so, furnish me with about three dol-
> lars or in the neighborhood of that sum as I am in
> much need of this timely help.
> Affectionately,
> Lucy Smith
> Mother in Israel

At the bottom of the note one finds written in the hand of Bishop Whitney, "Sent $5 by I. C. Kingsbury the evening I received this order."[25]

During the last conference of the Church held in Nauvoo, October 1845, Mother Smith was honored with a seat on the rostrum among the General Authorities. President Young invited her to address the conference, and she spoke at great length. From the minutes of the conference we have a brief summary of her talk:

> She commenced by saying that she was truly glad that the Lord had let her see so large a congregation. There were comparatively few in the assembly who were acquainted with her family. She was the mother of eleven children, seven of whom were boys (now all but one dead). She raised them in the fear and love of God, and never was there a more obedient family. She warned parents that they were accountable for their children's conduct; advised them to give them books and work to keep them from idleness; warned all to be full of love, goodness and kindness; and never to do in secret what they would not do in the presence of millions.[26]

When she inquired if the congregation would bestow upon her the title of "Mother in Israel," President Brigham Young arose and said, "All of you who consider Mother Smith a Mother in Israel signify it by saying 'yes.'" One unanimous "yes" echoed throughout the assembly. This was very pleasing to Mother Smith.

Among other interesting things she said at the conference was:

> I feel as though God were vexing this nation a little here and there, and I feel that the Lord will let Brother Brigham take the people away. Here in this city lay my dead—my husband and children, and if it so be that the rest of my children go with you (and I would to God that they may all go) they will not go without me; and if I go I want my bones brought back in case I die away, and deposited by my husband and children.

At the conclusion of her talk, President Young announced:

> Mother Smith proposes a thing which rejoices my heart. She will go with us. I can answer for the authorities of the Church, we want her and her children to go with us; and I pledge myself in behalf of the authorities of the Church, that while we have anything they shall share with us. We have extended the helping hand to Mother Smith. She has the best carriage in the city and while she lives shall ride in it and where she pleases . . . And I pledge myself, if Mother Smith goes with us and I outlive her, I will do my best to bring her bones back again and deposit them with her children, and I want to know if this people are willing to enter into a covenant to do the same. [The vote in the affirmative was unanimous.][27]

President Young was ever mindful of Mother Smith. He was anxious to help her and the other Smith widows travel to the Rocky Mountains with the faithful. When the whole family chose to stay behind (with the exception of Hyrum's widow and children), President Young pushed westward with a grieved heart, praying for Lucy and the rest of the Smith family. Fourteen months later on the eve of his departure from Winter Quarters with the vanguard of the pioneers, his thoughts were centered on Mother Smith. He wrote a lengthy letter to "Mrs. Lucy Smith, Beloved Mother in Israel." In it he said:

> Your memory and that of your dear husband, our Father in Israel, is sweet unto us, and ever will be, and that of all your household, whom the Lord has given unto you, for he has given you a family to increase without number, which shall continue without end.
> If our dear Mother Smith should at any time wish to come where the Saints are located, and she shall make it manifest to us, there is no sacrifice too great to bring her forward. Peace be to our Mother Smith, may her last days be her best days, and may the choicest blessings of Heaven and earth abide with you forever

is the prayer of your beloved children, in the name of Jesus Christ, Amen.[28]

Being batted about by diverse claims to church leadership, Lucy struggled. Still, she might have gone west had it not been for the conflict surrounding her only living son, William. William was excommunicated in October 1845 when he manifest a bitter spirit against the leaders of the Church. He succeeded in clouding the minds of his relatives, and the entire family were swayed to suspect the Twelve had complicity in the murders of Joseph and Hyrum. The whole family was set into confusion by William's ungrounded suspicions and their own feelings of distress.

Apparently these members of the Smith family having lost faith in the leadership were unable to discern the importance of the Church making the long trek into the unknown west. So William, Emma, the three sisters, and their children remained in Illinois. But years later these families were still in the Church and were visited by the brethren and relatives who traveled through. Only after 1860, when Joseph III became president of the Reorganized Church of Jesus Christ of Latter-day Saints did some of them "affiliate."

Mother Smith had her own conflict with the brethren when, after her son's excommunication, they admonished her that William, her only remaining son, should not be welcomed into her home.

William wanted to live with his mother, his wife having died. The agents were willing to support Mother Smith but not her son, William. They wrote to her: "You cannot expect to derive your support from the Church nor to have them make any provisions for you, if he is allowed to go on against the Church in your house." This grieved Lucy very much and in a long letter to Almon Babbitt, Joseph L. Heywood, and David Fulmer she stoutly protested such treatment: "You restrict my conscience, put limits to my affections, threaten me with poverty, if I do not drive my children from my doors because they resent insultance and abuse that has been heaped upon them without measure," she wrote.

She defended William: "As to William, he is my son and he has rights. As to the Twelve, you say they have rights, but who shall decide between them. Are you the judge?"[29]

Although she was furnished a comfortable home free of rent, she was given the home formerly owned by Joseph Noble. Mother Smith lived from time to time in the Mansion House or with her three married daughters, whose husbands manifest no real zeal in the cause of the restoration. (They would not have gone west with Mother Smith even if she had resolved to make the journey.)

Lucy had great inner struggle, but with so many of those she loved not willing to attempt the journey, perhaps it was not too difficult for the Prophet Joseph's aged mother to draw her shawl about her shoulders and sit in her rocking chair, and through tear-stained eyes gaze out the window to the covered wagons rolling down Water Street bearing the Saints to the Mississippi.

Mother Smith always seemed to manifest fervent interest in the true Church of Christ in the valleys of the mountains. Whenever an old friend visited her from Utah, she would inquire regarding the authorities and the progress of the Church. There was a time when she again seriously considered going West but age and ill health prevented her from carrying out her desire.

She often recalled that time when she was re-endowed the first day the temple was used for that purpose—December 10, 1845. Lucy had originally received her endowment 8 October 1843 in the mansion house, probably from Emma. With Mother Smith in the temple on that memorable occasion were other Smith widows, her daughters-in-law, Mary Fielding, and Agnes Coolbrith, son Don Carlos' widow. With Mary was her sister Mercy, and by Mother Smith stood her husband's brother, John, and his wife, Clarissa.

Mother Smith outlived her Prophet son by eleven years. Even though she was nearing four-score years at the time of her passing, she was alert in mind, body, and spirit, and could read the smallest print without glasses. Mother Smith spent her last years with her daughter-in-law Emma and Emma's second husband, Lewis Bidamon, in the Nauvoo Mansion House. Lucy moved there when she was 76. Lewis was kind and pleasant with their aging guest. He was a skilled crafts-man and fashioned for Mother Smith, who became an invalid, a couch on a carriage so that she could be wheeled about the house and yard. Emma made her mother-in-law absolutely welcome in her home. Lucy's own daughters could have shown her no greater love nor interest than Emma did.

Hannah Tapfield King visited Lucy a short while before her death and recorded these impressions of this aged Mother in Israel:

> We were shown into the room of Joseph's mother. She sat pillowed up in her bed. She made a great impression on me for she is no ordinary woman. I feel 'twould be in vain to try and describe my feelings towards her. I am going to let them turn into poetry, for prose would not suffice for me. She is a character that Walter Scott would have loved to portray, and one he would have done justice to; I do so in my heart where she shall have a niche for all time.
>
> She blessed us with a mother's blessing, her own words, and my heart melted for I remembered my own dear mother left England for the Gospel's sake, and deep fountains of my heart were broken up.[30]

In a volume of poems published by Mrs. King she did let her feelings run into poetry as she described her visit to the bedside of Mother Smith:

> Mother of Joseph! Yes, I've seen thy face,
> And felt thy kiss imprinted on my cheek;

And furthermore, with thy peculiar grace,
Thou blessed me with the blessings that I seek,
To thee, when 'ere He bids thy eyelids fall,
Short be thy slumber in the silent tomb;
The voice within my heart has but one call,
"Lord Jesus, come! Lord Jesus, quickly come!"

Oh then shalt thou again behold thy son!
Oh yes, thy sons Joseph, Hyrum—all;
Thy Samuel, too, whose hand thine eyes upon
Invoked the healing power of his call.
And by his priesthood—and 'twas sealed above,
In the bright courts where Christ gets gifts for men;

And when thy son removed his hand of love,
Those precious orbs were filled with light again.

O happy Mother, eternity shall tell
How blest thou art!—and now to thee farewell.[31]

On 5 May 1856, just two months before she would
have reached her four-score mark, Mother Smith fell
asleep in the Mansion House to awaken again in the
paradise of the blest. When word of her passing
reached the Saints in Utah, her nephew, Elder George
A. Smith, wrote an eloquent eulogy regarding this
noble mother, part of which follows:

> Blessed woman! Her name and memory are
> engraven upon the tablets of the hearts of tens of thou-
> sands; and will be handed down to millions yet
> unborn, who will speak her praise, and tell of her
> virtues and goodness, of her motherly kindness, her
> watchful care, and administration to the sick and
> afflicted—the kind and affectionate mother, the
> beloved wife, the partner of her aged and venerable
> husband—of her deeds of love, her virtue, faith, hope
> and confidence in God, the trials and persecution she
> bore for the Gospel of Truth, her unvarying steadfast-
> ness to truth through all circumstances; and being
> filled with charity for all, her God blessed her and

raised her up to bear the trials and persecutions she was called upon to undergo, and gave sufficient for her day, and in copious profusion, poured out His Holy Spirit upon her.

Few indeed, are the women that have ever lived or graced this lower world, that occupied the position she did. The chosen of the Lord, to bear and bring into the world one of the greatest Prophets the world ever produced. The *Millennial Star* printed this tribute to her:

> She was the wife, the partner of the earthly father of such sons and prophets. Her husband, a patriarch of the Most High over all the Church of God pouring out his blessings in the name of His Redeemer upon the heads of thousands by virtue of his priesthood and office, and causing their hearts to beat with joy. But her labors are closed and like a stock of corn fully ripe, she has gone down to her grave in peace, full of honor and goodness, there to await the morning of the first resurrection, after having lived to commit to the silent tomb, her husband, Joseph, Hyrum, Don Carlos, Samuel, etc.; but she has gone to meet them kings and priests to the Most High. Noble Mother in Israel! Blessed among women and queen among the mighty ones; thy calling and election has been made sure, and in the morning of the resurrection, with thy husband and offspring—no more to be separated, no more to endure persecution, trials, tears, pain and sorrows, but to bask in the smiles, fruition, and blessings of a celestial world, under the smiles of thy God and Redeemer, while eternity goes and eternity comes. Peace to her ashes. Amen.[32]

Notes

[1] Joseph Fielding Smith, op cit. p. 39.

[2] Joseph Smith, *History of the Church*, B. H. Roberts, ed. 2nd ed., rev. (Salt Lake City: Deseret Book, 1978) vol. 4:125-6.

[3] Lucy Mack Smith, p. 17.

[4] Smith, p. 32.

[5] *Ibid.*, p. 34.

[6] *Ibid.*, p. 63.

[7] *Ibid.*, p. 70

[8] B. H. Roberts, *A Comprehensive History of the Church* (Provo: BYU Press, 1965), Vol. 1, p. 40.

[9] Lucy Mack Smith, *History of Joseph Smith by his Mother*, (Stevens & Wallis Inc., 1945), p. 45.

[10] Walter C. Erdman, *Sources of Power in Famous Lives*, p. 135.

[11] Smith, p. 204.

[12] Smith, p. 216.

[13] *Journal of History*, Reorganized Church of Jesus Christ of Latter-day Saints, vol. 1:409.

[14] Andrew Jenson, *Biographical Encyclopedia* (Salt Lake City: Andrew Jenson History Company, 1920), 1:691.

[15] History of the Church, Vol. 3, p. 175.

[16] Luck Mack Smith, p. 291.

[17] *Ibid.*, p. 229.

[18] Smith, pp. 265-66.

[19] Jenson, p. 691.

[20] Josiah Quincy, *Figures of the Past, From the Leaves of an Old Journal* (Boston: Roberts Brothers, 1883), p. 386.

[21] E. Cecil McGavin, *Nauvoo the Beautiful* (Salt Lake City, Utah: Stevens & Wallis Inc., 1946), p. 144.

[22] Smith, p. 278.

[23] McGavin.

[24] Matthias F. Cowley, *Wilford Woodruff* (Salt Lake City, Utah: Bookcraft, 1964), p. 228.

[25] McGavin.

[26] B. H. Roberts, *Comprehensive History of the Church*, 6 vols. (Provo, Utah: Brigham Young University Press, 1965), 2:539. Hereafter cited as CHC.

[27] CHC 2:529.

[28] Journal History, April 4, 1847 (Primary History of the Church).

[29] Milo M. Quaife, *The Kingdom of St. James* (New Haven, Conn., 1930), p. 246.

[30] McGavin, p. 81.

[31] Hannah Tapfield King, *Volume of Poems*, 1846.

[32] *Millennial Star* 18: 559.

Emma Hale Smith:
The Elect Lady

The importance of Emma Hale Smith in the rise of the Church is emphasized in a revelation given through Joseph the Seer in Harmony, Susquehanna County, Pennsylvania, in July 1830. The Lord tells the Seer's wife: "And thou art an elect lady, whom I have called." (Doctrine and Covenants 25:3.) In this important revelation, which is the only formal revelation given to a woman in this dispensation, this remarkable woman was also ordained to "expound scriptures and to exhort the Church, according as it shall be given thee" by the Spirit of the Lord. She was to give time to writing and to "learning much." Emma was enjoined to "lay aside the things of the world and seek for the things of a better" and to comfort her husband "in his afflictions with consoling words, in the spirit of meekness." She was assured by the Lord that "thy husband shall support thee in the Church."

In a very impressive way Emma fulfilled all that was required of her, as wife of the Prophet Joseph Smith, until his death. Only then did she draw back, seemingly to turn her back on all her husband had performed. Therefore for more than a century she has been a controversial figure in the history of the Church.

Emma was devotedly attached to her husband. She endured hardship, persecution, and heartache for his sake; and she did it all without a murmur. She took life and its vicissitudes cheerfully. Lucy Smith, her mother-in-law, said of Emma: "I have never seen a woman in my life, who would endure every species of fatigue and hardship, from month to month, and from year to year, with that unflinching courage, zeal, and patience to endure. She has been tossed on the ocean of uncertainty; she has breasted the storms of persecution and buffeted the rage of men and devils, which would have borne down almost any other woman."[1]

An incident which occurred during the summer of 1842 is indicative of Emma's support of her husband. At that time Joseph was being accused of being an accessory in an attempted assassination of Lilburn Boggs, former governor in Missouri.

Frustrated with the unjust harassment he was under, Joseph went into hiding, and seriously considered fleeing to the Pine Woods country in what is now Wisconsin, for safety. But he would not go without his beloved Emma. He wrote to her asking her to prepare to go, if need be. On August 1842, Emma sent this reply to him in his exile: "I am ready to go with you if you are obliged to leave; and Hyrum says he will go with me. I shall make the best arrangements I can and be as well prepared as possible . . . Yours affectionately forever, Emma Smith."[2]

Joseph's love for Emma was equally fervent. Following a visit of Emma to him during his island exile, the Prophet rose to poetic expression in these endearing sentiments:

> What unspeakable delight, and what transport of joy swelled my bosom, when I took by the hand, on that night, my beloved Emma—she that was my wife, even the wife of my youth and the choice of my heart. Many were the vibrations of my mind when I contemplated for a moment the many scenes we had been called to

pass through, the fatigues and the toil, the sorrows and sufferings, and the joys and the consolations, from time to time, which had strewn our paths and crowned our board. Oh, what a commingling of thoughts filled my mind for the moment! And again she is here, even in the seventh trouble—undaunted, firm and unwavering, unchangeable, affectionate Emma.[3]

Emma was of English descent, the third daughter and seventh child in a family of nine. She was born in Harmony (now Oakland,) Pennsylvania, 10 July 1804. Emma's mother, Elizabeth Lewis, was a sister of a renowned Methodist minister. One of her neighbors once said of her, "I never visited her but I thought I learned something useful."[4]

Emma's father, Isaac Hale, a well established farmer, innkeeper, and noted hunter in Susquehanna County was also a veteran of the Revolutionary War. He seems to have been remembered most for his hunting, for the epitaph on his grave reads, "The body of Isaac Hale, the hunter, like the cover of an old book, its contents torn out and stripped of its lettering and gilding, lies here."[5]

A descendant writing of Emma observes: "With four older brothers and one younger, Emma grew up in an environment of easy camaraderie. She was a skilled horsewoman and enjoyed many outdoor activities such as canoeing with her brothers on the Susquehanna River, which was not far from their home. She was fond of her brothers and sisters and throughout her tempestuous life she tried to maintain contact with them. She had an especially close bond with her father. According to family tradition, he was converted to Christianity by overhearing Emma's prayer for him when she was only six years old."[6]

She probably received most of her schooling in the vicinity. However, she went away from home for one year where she completed a year's training at a girls' school. It is said of her that she "never used slang and was very particular about her grammar and choice of words." She was noted as a meticulous housekeeper and an excellent cook; and, after moving to Illinois and into a permanent home of her own, she was celebrated far and wide as a most gracious hostess. Her early home environment prepared her well for that role. The Hales lived in prosperity and enjoyed many cultural and social advantages. Their inn was a respected establishment in the community. It was there that twenty-one-year old Emma first met Joseph.

When young Joseph Smith was employed by Josiah Stoal of Chenango County, New York, he boarded at the Hales. There he met the dark-eyed Emma. From the descriptions left of her by her contempories she was a beautiful young woman. Emma was tall, well proportioned, dignified in body, with "bewitching dark eyes."[7]

Following a brief courtship, Joseph returned to Manchester when his employment with Mr. Stoal terminated. Shortly after his arrival home, he confided to his mother and father his intention to marry Emma: "I have concluded to get married and if you have no objections to my uniting myself in marriage with Miss Emma Hale, she would be my choice in preference to any other woman I have ever met." Father and Mother Smith were pleased with his choice and readily consented to his marriage.[8] When Joseph asked permission of Emma's father, Isaac Hale flatly refused his consent, telling Joseph plainly that he was a stranger who had no steady employment, one who had the reputation of being a peep-stone gazer and a hunter for buried treasure, all of which practical minded old Isaac Hale would not countenance.

But Emma loved Joseph and, in her own words, preferred "to marry him to any other man I knew." The Prophet informs us that he was "under the necessity of taking her elsewhere (to be married); so we went and were married at the house of Squire Tarbill in South

Bainbridge, Chenango County, New York"[9] Call this an elopement if you will, but both he and Emma were of age and knew what they were about, Emma being a year and a half older than Joseph. "Whatever attraction drew Joseph and Emma together, it was sufficient to hold them through depth of privation, persecution and trials, committed to each other and their sacred mission from the day of their marriage in January 1827, until the day seventeen years later when the Prophet was felled by assassins' bullets.

> Unwittingly, Emma had become the wife of the man God had chosen to head the Dispensation of the Fullness of Times. Nobody knows what Emma's feelings were concerning Joseph's prophetic gifts at the time of their marriage. However, the record shows— by her constancy through trial— Emma's ultimate conviction that he was a prophet of God.[10]

A historian of Susquehanna County shared the view of the Hales regarding Emma's marriage to young Joseph: "Their daughter, Emma, was intelligent, and that she should marry Joseph Smith, Jr., the Mormon leader, can only be accounted for by supposing he had bewitched her as he afterwards bewitched the masses."[11] But Emma did not think so.

Emma went with her husband the night he received the golden plates from the Angel Moroni. According to Mother Smith, Emma came into the room after midnight on the morning of September 22, in her riding dress; and shortly thereafter she and Joseph rode to the Hill Cumorah in Joseph Knight's wagon. They returned later that morning and Joseph confided to his mother that he had hidden the plates in the woods. Later the plates were brought home. Emma was closely associated with the translation of the Book of Mormon, acting for a short time as the Prophet's scribe; and yet she was never given the privilege of seeing the golden plates.

When she was an elderly woman, her son Joseph III asked her, "Mother, what is your belief about the authenticity or origin of the Book of Mormon?" She answered:

> My belief is that the Book of Mormon is of divine authenticity: I have not the slightest doubt of it; I am sat-isfied that no man could have dictated the writing of the manuscript unless he was inspired: for, when I was act-ing as his scribe, your father would dictate to me hour after hour; and when returning after meals, or after interruptions, he would at once begin where he had left off, without either seeing the manuscript or having any portion of it read to him. It would have been improbable that a learned man could do this; and, for one so . . . unlearned as he was, it was simply impossible.[12]

During an attempt made by unscrupulous people to steal the plates, Emma rode ten miles on horseback to warn Joseph of danger, and this at a time when she was pregnant with her first child. Not many weeks after this, through her influence, Isaac Hale sent his son, Alva, with team and wagon, and she and Joseph moved to Harmony where the Prophet bought thirteen acres of land from his father-in-law and began to farm. At every opportunity he would study the sacred records.

A friend, Martin Harris, came to write for him so he could translate the record, and they had a portion of the manuscript translated by June of 1828. Emma was about to give birth to her first child, and Martin planned to return to Palmyra to do his spring work, so he prevailed upon Joseph to let him take the 116 page manuscript home to Palmyra, to help him convince his wife to finance the printing. During his absence, Emma gave birth to little Alva, who died shortly after his birth. Emma herself hovered between life and death. Joseph did not leave her bedside for two weeks, watching over, caring for, and praying for his beloved Emma.

Somehow Martin lost the manuscript, and it was

quite some time before Oliver Cowdery came along to serve as scribe so Joseph could continue with the translation. When it was finally completed, Martin Harris was true to his word, and financed the printing of the Book of Mormon which came off the press in 1829. Emma considered this a "marvelous work and a wonder" as much to her as to anybody else.[13]

The Church was organized 6 April 1830, and the following winter, Joseph and Emma moved to Ohio to establish a safer and better place from which to send the gospel to the world. Emma had buried her first baby, Alva, in Pennsylvania, in 1828; in Ohio Emma gave birth to twins, Thaddeus and Louisa, who only lived three hours. Shortly thereafter, a member of the church, Julia Clapp Murdock, died after giving birth to twins. Their father, John Murdock, could not take care of the infants, so Joseph had him bring the babies to Emma to nurse. They later adopted them.

These babies brought joy to Emma, but in March of 1831, a mob broke into their bedroom in Hiram, Ohio, taking Joseph out into the night to beat him, and cover him with tar. Exposure to the cold caused little Joseph Murdock, who was sick with the measles, to get pneumonia. He died a few days later. Little Julia Murdock survived, and was reared as their adopted daughter. In 1832, Joseph had to make a trip to New York City, Albany, and Boston, thus having to be away before Emma was to give birth again. Emma's apprehension must have been extreme, and Joseph, sensitive to her fears, wrote to her from New York City:

> I returned to my room to meditate and to calm my mind, and behold the thought of home, of Emma and Julia rushed upon my mind like a flood, and I could wish for a moment to be with them. My breast is filled with all the feelings and the tenderness of a parent and a husband and could I be with you, I would tell you many things . . . .

I feel as if I wanted to say something to comfort you in your peculiar trial and present afflictions. I hope God will give you strength that you will not faint. I pray to God to soften the hearts around you to be kind to you and to take the burden off your shoulders as much as possible. You must comfort yourself knowing God is your friend and that you have one true and living friend on earth, your husband.[14]

Young Joseph III, born 6 November 1832 was a healthy survivor. Three years later another healthy son, Frederick Granger Williams, was born in 20 June 1836, about six weeks after the dedication of the Kirtland Temple. Two years later, Joseph and Emma were forced to flee Kirtland for Far West, where three months after their arrival plump Alexander Hale was born 2 June 1838. Emma, known for her wit, remarked the night this little son was born that a "Halestorm was in progress."

Of the nine children born to Emma, only four lived. Don Carlos was born in Nauvoo 13 June 1840, and died 15 August 1841. A stillborn son born 26 December 1842 is buried in Nauvoo.

Emma embraced the Church founded 6 April 1830, by her husband. She was baptized for the remission of her sins, by Oliver Cowdery, 28 June 1830, in a pond made by damming a stream of water near Joseph Knight's house in Colesville, New York. Due to persecution, it was not until early August that she was confirmed a member of the Church. In the revelation referred to before and given in July 1830, the Lord assured her that her husband should soon confirm her a member of the Church. "For he shall lay his hands upon thee, and thou shalt receive the Holy Ghost." (D&C 25:8.) Newel Knight and his wife, Sally, were visiting them at Harmony. Joseph planned to confirm the two women and to administer the sacrament for the group before they left for Colesville. Regarding this important occasion the Prophet recorded that after being warned of the Lord not to buy wine from their enemies:

We prepared some wine of our own making, and held our meeting consisting of only five, viz., Newel Knight and his wife, myself and my wife, and John Whitmer. We partook together of the sacrament, after which we confirmed these two sisters into the Church and spent the evening in a glorious manner. The Spirit of the Lord was poured out upon us, we praised the Lord God, and rejoiced exceedingly.[15]

Emma's life was filled with trials. She was driven from her home three times. On two of these flights she was forced to depart without her husband. Once he had fled for his life, and the second time he was unjustly taken to prison. When little Alexander was six months old, the Prophet was ruthlessly taken from her by the heartless mob who were posing as Missouri Militia; and it was only after much entreaty that he was permitted to return to his sorrowing family for a brief farewell. Joseph the Prophet wrote of this touching scene of departure:

I found my wife and children in tears, who feared that we had been shot by those who had sworn to take our lives, and that they would see me no more. When I entered my house, they clung to my garments their eyes streaming with tears, mingled emotions of joy and sorrow were manifested in their countenances. I requested to have a private interview with them for a few minutes, but this privilege was denied me by the guard. I was then obliged to take my departure. Who can realize the feelings which I experienced at that time, to be thus torn from my companion, and leave her surrounded with monsters in the shape of men, and my children, too, not knowing how their wants would be supplied; while I was to be taken far from them in order that my enemies might destroy me when they thought proper to do so. My partner wept, my children clung to me, until they were thrust from me by the swords of the guards. I felt overwhelmed while I witnessed the scene, and could only recommend them to the care of that God whose kindness had followed me to the present time, and who alone could protect them, and deliver me from the hands of my enemies, and restore me to my family.[16]

Joseph had cause for concern. Emma was not well, and the oldest of the four children was six years old. She was left without protection and at the mercy of the mob who came into Far West after the surrender of the Church leaders. This mob appropriated anything and everything they saw, whipping the men, abusing the children, and violating some women.

As a prisoner in chains from a dingy dungeon in Richmond, Missouri, the Prophet Joseph wrote to his beloved Emma:

> O God grant that I may have the privilege of seeing once again my lovely family, in the enjoyment of the sweets of liberty and social life; to press them to my bosom and kiss their lovely cheeks would fill my heart with unspeakable gratitude.
>
> Oh, my affectionate Emma, I want you to remember that I am a true and faithful friend to you, and the children forever. Oh, may God bless you all![17]

Emma shared and endured much tribulation with her sisters in the faith. We seldom realize that at least 15,000 people were driven unmercifully from their homes. Hyrum Smith in reviewing the tragic exodus from Missouri referred to the losses of Emma in these words: "His (Joseph's) family also were robbed of all they had, and barely escaped with the skin of their teeth."[18]

Yet during this time of suffering, danger, and death, Emma journeyed three times to visit and comfort her husband at the jail in Liberty, Clay County, Missouri, where he was incarcerated. Although Emma and the wives of other brethren who were fellow prisoners with the Prophet arrived in Liberty 1 December 1839, it was not until December 8th that they were permitted to visit the jail and spend a night with their husbands.

When she was not traveling to see her husband, Emma was caring for her four children in a city where there was little food except dried corn. When word came that Joseph needed blankets, she wept, for she had none to send him.

"The suffering of the Church members at that time cannot be adequately described. It was obvious that the only thing they could do was comply as quickly as possible with the order to leave the state."[19]

A committee of seven men was appointed to supervise the move. "The committee for removal decided that the first families to be moved were those of the presidency and the other prisoners. Then every effort would be made to get every man, woman and child who wanted to leave Missouri, out of the state. When Emma had visited Joseph in Liberty Jail on January 20, Sheriff Hadley told her that if she would leave the state, he thought Joseph might be released within a short time."[20]

The Prophet Joseph was also anxious to have his wife moved from the frightful scenes in Missouri. Stephen Markham was appointed an agent for the Church to raise the means to assist the exiled Saints to migrate to a place of safety; and while the Prophet was languishing in the Liberty Jail, Emma and her children were being helped out of Missouri into Illinois. He joined her there in April, after a daring escape.

In Illinois the Saints built Nauvoo. During the Nauvoo period of the Church, Emma enjoyed some peaceful and pleasant days. She shared with her prophet-husband the joys of witnessing the building of the "city beautiful" and the gathering of the Saints to Nauvoo. There were days when Joseph was at home to converse with her and play with the children. On parade days she rode by the side of her handsome husband who, as lieutenant general, led the Nauvoo Legion.

One finds such entries in the Prophet's journal as "Spent the day at home conversing with Emma" and "This day Emma began to be sick with fever, conse-

quently I kept in the house with her all day." Six days
later he entered, "My dear Emma was worse. Many
fears were entertained that she would not recover. She
was baptized twice in the river, which evidently did her
much good. She grew worse again at night and continued very sick indeed. I was unwell and much troubled
on account of Emma's sickness." But the next day:
"Emma is better; may the Lord speedily raise her to the
bosom of her family, that the heart of His servant may
be comforted again."[21]

One of the highlights of Emma's life came on 17 March
1842 when she was elected by her peers, president of the
Church's organization for the women, the Relief Society.
The organization took place upstairs in the Red Brick Store,
and was under the direction of the Prophet Joseph Smith,
assisted by John Taylor and Willard Richards. The question
was raised, "What shall this society be called?" A discus-
sion ensued, with the proposal that it be called "The
Nauvoo Female Relief Society." John Taylor offered an
amendment that it be called the "Nauvoo Female
Benevolent Society," a title that he thought would give a
more definite and extended meaning to the society. Emma
reasoned with John Taylor on the words "relief and benevolent." Joseph agreed with Taylor that "benevolent" had
an ameliorative connotation where as "relief" might be
misconstrued, moreover "benevolent" was a popular term.

"The popularity of the word "benevolent," protested Emma, "is one great objection." She reminded her
husband of the corrupt Washington Benevolent Society.
"Certainly, we would not want anyone to associate the
organized womanhood of Nauvoo with a group so
tainted." Other sisters concurred with Emma and
added that the daughters of Zion should be an example
for all the world and not follow courses heretofore pursued. Then Emma added: We are going to do
something extraordinary—when a boat is stuck on the
rapids with a multitude of Mormons on board we shall

consider that a loud call for relief. We expect extraordinary occasions and pressing calls."[22]

John Taylor arose and shook his head, "I shall have to concede the point—your arguments are so potent. I cannot stand before them. I shall have to give way." And so the society to be presided over by Sister Emma Smith was called "The Female Relief Society of Nauvoo."[23] Emma was a most acceptable leader and was honored and respected by the women of the Church, women who were described by the Prophet as being "our most intelligent, humane, philanthropic and respectable ladies. . . . They will fly to the relief of the stranger; they will pour in oil and wine to the wounded heart of the distressed; they will dry up the tears of the orphan and make the widow's heart to rejoice. Our women have always been signalized for the acts of benevolence and kindness."[24] And the leader in these charitable deeds was Emma.

On the occasion of her calling, the Prophet Joseph explained that "an elect lady" was one who was elected to do a certain work in the Church. He explained that with Emma's being elected president of the Relief Society organization, the revelation regarding Emma in D&C 25:3 was fulfilled.[25] It was not because she was the wife of the Latter-day Seer that the Lord favored her with this calling, but because she was one who had received the gospel and was well-qualified for the work which God had foreordained her to accomplish in mortality.

In the same revelation, verses 11 and 12, Emma was given a special duty, "to make a selection of sacred hymns" for the Church. "For," said the Lord, "my soul delighteth in the song of the heart; yea, the song of the righteous is a prayer unto me and it shall be answered with a blessing upon their heads." (D&C 25:12.) Next to scriptures, hymns present one of the most powerful statements of doctrine in the Church. Selection of hymns for this purpose was a grave responsibility.

Many a soul has had Mormonism brought to him by a
peculiarly Mormon hymn; and Emma was the one designated to establish the pattern by selecting the first hymns
for the Church. More than five years would pass between
her calling to make a collection of hymns for the Church,
and the completion of the little book of 90 hymns, with
words only. On the title page of her hymnal was printed:
"A Collection of Sacred Hymns for the Church of the
Latter-day Saints, selected by Emma Smith, Kirtland,
Ohio, Printed by F. G. Williams and Company, 1835."

It is interesting to note in passing that she grouped
and classified the hymns. There were hymns on baptism,
on the sacrament, on marriage, and on various other top-
ics. Many of these hymns included in that first hymnal
are in the current hymnbooks; still among our favorites
include: "How Firm a Foundation," "I Know That My
Redeemer Lives," and "Arise, My Soul, Arise."

During the five years Emma labored to collect the
hymns she and Joseph moved to Ohio where they lived
for a time at the Morley settlement, then at Hiram, in
the John Johnson home, and then settled above the
Whitney Store in Kirtland. Later they lived in a log
home near the Chagrin River at Kirtland. She went with
Joseph to the frontier of Missouri, and finally to Illinois.

One occasion of delight in Emma's life occurred when
Joseph was free to take her and the children on a long trip
to visit Emma's sister, Elizabeth Wasson, who lived at
Dixon. This is the only long trip Joseph took with his wife
for pleasure, and one can imagine that it was enjoyable to
both. They no sooner arrived at the Wassons, however,
when kidnappers from Missouri, arrived and captured
Joseph. They threw him into a wagon and Emma had just
time to toss him his hat and coat, as they raced away with
him, leaving her and the children stranded. They made
their way back to Nauvoo with the help of Emma's
nephew. Friends of the Prophet rescued him from his kidnappers and he was safely returned to Nauvoo. And

what an occasion his return was! As he and his friends neared Nauvoo, they were met by half the city who with tears of joy had come out to meet and greet their leader. In the lead of this multitude were Emma and Hyrum Smith. Joseph hurriedly got out of the buggy in which he was riding and, "after embracing Emma and my brother Hyrum, who wept tears of joy at my return. . . . I mounted my favorite horse, Old Charley, when the band struck up "Hail Columbia," and proceeded to march slowly towards the city, Emma riding by my side into town." and how his family embraced him and rejoiced over his safe return! He says, "My children clung around me with feelings of enthusiastic and enraptured pleasure. Little Fred exclaimed, "Pa, the Missourians won't take you away again, will they?"[26]

Emma was a marvelous cook. In the Mansion House, friends often gathered to enjoy the delicious food prepared by the gracious hostess. On 18 January 1843, she and Joseph commemorated their sixteenth wedding anniversary by serving four tables of guests. They had a wonderful celebration that lasted until two in the morning.

One time William W. Phelps was dining with them. Emma was serving the meal. While the dinner was being served, the Prophet remarked to Phelps what a kind, provident wife he had. When he wanted a little bread and milk, she would load the table with so many good things it would destroy his appetite. William suggested that the Prophet should be like Bonaparte —"have a little table, just large enough for the victuals you want yourself." Emma entered the room at that point and said, "Mr. Smith is a bigger man than Bonaparte: he can never eat without his friends." And the Prophet remarked to Emma, "That is the wisest thing I ever heard you say."[27] Emma enjoyed cooking for his friends and serving them.

Emma was a meticulous housekeeper and an ambitious, tireless worker. She was always tidy and neat about her appearance: "When her afternoon work was done, Emma would recomb and redress her hair for the rest of the day; she was always very neat."[28]

For many years, Joseph and Emma seemed to have had an understanding that their relationship was eternal, often signing their letters, "forever" and "eternally yours." They looked forward to the completion of the temple where sacred sealing ordinances would be performed. However, by the end of April 1843 the temple was not done, and the Prophet felt a great urgency to finish laying the foundation of the organization of the Church. Therefore, Emma's home became the scene of sacred ordinance work.[29]

According to Brigham Young, "In the Old Homestead on 28 May 1843, Hyrum sealed Emma to Joseph in the new and everlasting covenant. The Prophet had previously performed marriages, uniting other couples for time and all eternity; now, through the power vested in the Priesthood, he had claim upon Emma throughout all the time here and the eternities hereafter."[30]

Later, in the fall, the Prophet administered sacred ordinances to Emma, and she received the blessings of the fullness of the priesthood with Joseph, in the upstairs room of their newly completed Mansion House. "This was not done with pomp or circumstance, but quietly, and in privacy. She was the first woman in this dispensation to receive these blessings."[31]

Emma became the first female ordinance worker in the Church. Under the Prophet, she gave many a sister anointings and assisted with other ceremonies of the endowment both in the upper room of her husband's store and in a specially set-apart room in the Mansion House. Bathsheba B. Smith, wife of George A. Smith, tells of receiving ordinances in Sister Emma Smith's home and that she and her husband received their endowments in the upper room of the Prophet's store.[32]

"Throughout the year of 1843 and into the early part of 1844, Emma presided, under Joseph's direction, over the administration of these sacred ordinances for women. She herself administered the washing and anointing to Joseph's mother, Lucy, to Mary Fielding Smith, and according to Heber C. Kimball's journal, to his wife Vilate, and "meny [sic] other females."[33]

Joseph and Emma, with their family lived for only ten months together in the Mansion House before the martyrdom. Emma enjoyed the beauty, comfort and security of that lovely home. Most of her seventeen years of married life had been spent in the homes of friends or in small houses amidst poverty, persecution, and privation. Now, oh, what a joy and contrast.

Joseph dictated in his history that their home had been a resting place for thousands, "and our family many times obliged to do without food, after having fed all we had to visitors; and could have continued the same liberal course, had it not been for the cruel and untiring persecution of my relentless enemies. We have provided the best table accommodations in the city, and the Mansion being large and convenient, renders travelers more comfortable than any other place on the upper Mississippi."[34] Thus Emma's new home became a hotel.

A close associate of Joseph and Emma was Benjamin F. Johnson. He once observed, "As a husband and father, his (Joseph's) devotion to wife and children stopped only at idolatry. His life's greatest motive after God and kingdom was that of wife, children and friends." One Sunday morning as Benjamin and Joseph sat together in the front room of the Mansion House, two of Joseph's sons came running to him, both freshly cleaned and washed with their Sunday clothes on. As Joseph gathered them in his lap, he exclaimed, "Benjamin, look at these boys, how can I help but love their mother. Why I'd go to hell for such a woman."[35]

The biggest trial in the life of the "Elect Lady" came when her husband introduced into the Church the doctrine embracing plurality of wives. Emma was very much tried by this principle. Orson Pratt tells us that Emma "was embittered against Joseph, and at times fought against him with all her heart; then again she would break down in her feelings, and humble herself, and would lead forth ladies and place their hands in the hands of her husband, and they were married to him according to the law of God."[36]

A serving girl in the Mansion House recalled overhearing Joseph and Emma talking and then Emma crying. Joseph called the girl, Maria Jane Woodward, and asked her to go to Hyrum's home and ask him to come. When Hyrum arrived, he went into the room, and Jane heard Hyrum say, "Well, Sister Emma, what is the matter?" Jane heard nothing more. The following day, as Jane was working upstairs making beds, Emma came up and said,

> "It was you that Joseph came to when he sent for Hyrum last night was it?" I said, "Yes, Ma'am." Then she told me to sit down on the bed by her and we both sat down on the bed that I was making. She looked very sad and cast down, and then she said to me, "The principle of plural marriage is right, but I am like other women, I am naturally jealous hearted and can talk back to Joseph as long as any wife can talk back to her husband, but what I want to say to you is this. You heard me finding fault with the principle. I want to say that the principle is right, it is from our Father in Heaven," and then she again spoke of her jealousy . . . "What I said I have got (to) repent of. The principle is right but I am jealous hearted. Now never tell anybody that you heard me find fault with Joseph of that principle. The principle is right and if I or you or anyone else finds fault with that principle we have got to humble ourselves and repent of it."[37]

Emma rightly feared that the introduction of this principle would bring destruction upon her husband in the world, yet she knew it was an essential part of the restoration of the Dispensation of the Fullness of times. The paradox of her life lies in the fact that in later years, when the brethren in Utah publically acknowledged the doctrine, Emma denied ever having known of or participating in any such thing. This outraged Brigham Young, John Taylor, and the others who had been witnesses to her participation in it during Joseph's lifetime. Perhaps her denials can only be understood in light of the tragedy she suffered, and her fateful decision not to move west with the Church when it left Nauvoo in 1846. Living as she was in that environment among people who would not understand or care, it would have been easier for Emma to deny it than explain it.

In the spring of 1844 Joseph recognized that his enemies were apt to take his life soon. He was being called a "fallen prophet" by some of his own circle, but he insisted he was not. He told his friends that though he was as apt to err as any man, there was nothing wrong in the revelations.

"Emma heard the words—she saw the clouds of the gathering storm—she worried and struggled with her own crisis, another baby coming, a hotel to run, an increasing awareness that she and Joseph would never know peace on this earth. . . . Perhaps she had come to believe that he was impervious to danger. He was, after all, God's anointed prophet. Just as she had faith that no one could molest the golden plates, she must have believed that God would look after His own."[38]

The temple was under construction, rising high on the hill above the Mississippi River. The city was growing, absorbing hundreds of converts from England, Canada, and all over the United States. Missionaries were going to the American Indians, the people of the Islands, and Orson Hyde had dedicated the Holy Land to the gathering of the Jews. Emma presided over a Relief Society with membership numbered in the thousands.

"In May of 1844 Emma was in the third month of her pregnancy. Most of the time she was too ill to go about her work and had to remain in bed. Joseph cancelled his engagements and stayed with her as much as possible. No doubt they worried over the possibility of her losing this baby, also."[39]

Joseph's enemies publicly declared him a fallen prophet and a close associate filed charges against him, which he was required to answer in Carthage on May 27th. The mob spirit was apparent. "The indictment was deferred until the next term of the court. Joseph went back to Nauvoo after a round trip of about thirty miles on horseback and a day spent in constant tension, with threats and warnings that his life was in danger. He arrived home about 9 p.m. and found Emma sick."[40]

The legal conflict escalated when, acting as Mayor of Nauvoo, Joseph instructed the Sheriff and a posse to destroy a newspaper press, *The Nauvoo Expositor*, which was spewing out vile accusations and inciting a mob spirit against the leaders of the Church. This action gave the enemies what they were looking for, a cause to bring Joseph back to Carthage for trial. Joseph knew the murderous intentions of his enemies and could see no other possibility for safety but for himself and Hyrum to escape from Nauvoo by crossing into Iowa Territory. They successfully crossed the Mississippi, but Hiram Kimball and Lorenzo Wasson entreated them to return. They brought a letter from Emma, purportedly urging him to return also, and Joseph and Hyrum crossed back into Illinois, with the intent to go to Carthage and the fate that awaited them there.

Mercy Thompson recorded seeing the skiff coming across the river, and watching as the men walked up to Hyrum's house. She said that Joseph waited while

Hyrum gathered his things and then the two of them went to the Mansion House. In Emma's later years, answering questions about this time when Joseph came back across the river, she said, "I felt the worst I ever felt in my life, from that time I looked for him to be killed."[41] Witnesses who saw Emma and Joseph's farewell as he left for Carthage said that she was "beyond consolation."

Prior to his leaving, Emma had asked Joseph for a blessing, but there was no time for him to give her one. He sent her word that if she would write the best blessing she could think of, he would sign it upon his return.

The blessing Emma wrote shows plainly how strongly she desired to measure up to every test of her faith and endure to the end of her mortal sojourn on earth, how greatly she prized wisdom and discernment, and her desire to accept God's revelations given through her husband, without doubting:

First of all, I would crave as the richest of heaven's blessings wisdom from my Heavenly Father bestowed daily, so that whatever I might do or say, I could not look back at the close of the day with regret, nor neglect the performance of any act that would bring a blessing. I desire the Spirit of God to know and understand myself, that I might be able to overcome whatever of tradition or nature that would not tend to my exaltation in the eternal worlds. I desire a fruitful, active mind, that I may be able to comprehend the designs of God, when revealed through His servants without doubting. I desire the spirit of discernment, which is one of the promised gifts of the Holy Ghost. I particularly desire wisdom to bring up all the children that are or may be committed to my charge, in such a manner that they will be useful ornaments in the kingdom of God, and in a coming day rise up and call me blessed. I desire prudence that I may not through ambition abuse my body and cause it to become old and care-worn, but that I may wear a cheerful countenance, living to perform all the work that I covenanted to perform in the spirit world and be a blessing to all who may need aught at my hands. I desire with all my heart to honor and respect my husband as my head, ever to live in his confidence and by acting in unison with him retain the place which God has given me by his side, and I ask my Heavenly Father that through humility I may be enabled to overcome the curse which was pronounced upon the daughters of Eve. I desire the blessings which God has in store for all who are willing to be obedient to His requirements. Finally, I desire that whatever may be my lot through life I may be enabled to acknowledge the hand of God in all things.[42]

Joseph was never able to return to sign this blessing because Emma's worst fears were realized when on the afternoon of June 27, her husband and brother-in-law, Hyrum, were shot and killed, while in protective custody in the upstairs apartment of the jailer in Carthage, Illinois. John Taylor was seriously wounded, and Willard Richards was left to send messages to Nauvoo informing the Saints of the terrible news. The death of the Prophet and Patriarch filled the Mansion with deep sorrow and lamentation. By daybreak hundreds of Saints loitered nearby awaiting the arrival of the bodies of the martyrs. When the wagon driven by Emma's brother-in-law, Samuel, arrived at the Mansion the lifeless bodies of the leaders were carried into the house and the door was closed. The next day thousands would file through the room where the bodies lay in state. All the Saints were devastated, and came to pay their last respects.

Perhaps on no occasion did Emma's love for Joseph appear stronger than when the bodies of the martyrs were brought to the Mansion House. Among the many who came to offer words of comfort was John P. Greene, an old friend, and one of the early converts to the Church. He was himself overcome with emotion and could only say, "O Sister Emma, God bless and comfort."

At length Emma sobbed, "Why, O God! am I thus afflicted? Why am I a widow and my children orphans? Thou knowest I have always trusted in thy law." Brother Greene tried to comfort her with the assurance that her afflictions would be to her a crown of life. She answered quickly, "My husband was my crown; for him and my children I have suffered the loss of all things; and why, O God, am I thus deserted, and my bosom torn with this ten fold anguish?"[43] The statement, "My husband was my crown," explains much about Emma and her course in life following the awful tragedy at Carthage.

Dimick B. Huntington escorted the sorrowing widow into the room where the coffins were placed. He held his wide-brimmed hat in front of Emma's face to shield her view of Joseph until she was directly in front of the bodies of Joseph and Hyrum. She fainted three times before she finally fell down beside Joseph, kissed his face, calling him by name, pleading for him to speak to her once more, to forgive her. No one could doubt Emma's sincere and eternal love for Joseph.

Emma was two weeks short of her 41st birthday. She was nearly four months along in her pregnancy, and had four children ages 13, 11, 8 and 6 to care for. She had buried six precious infants in three states. In the past she had endured poverty, privations and misery cheerfully, knowing that Joseph was there to protect her.[44]

In the aftermath of the murder of the Prophet, confusion was everywhere. "The question of who would lead the Church was on everyone's mind; there was no lack of volunteers. Sidney Rigdon felt he was the logical one, since he was a counselor in the presidency of the Church. William Marks, already in charge of the stake in Nauvoo was another choice. Brigham Young, the President of the Twelve, did not arrive back in the city until the flames of expectation had risen to a great height.

"During the heated debates, Emma was frequently approached for support. Her position as Joseph's widow placed her in a vulnerable role. Her word was sought. Ambitious pretenders for leadership often used her name unscrupulously to give their position prestige. This placed her in a danger she was not wary enough to perceive. "Always having been one to speak her thoughts freely, she continued to do so, and was often quoted (and misquoted) whether what she said was substantial or merely her own speculation, as she, too, wondered what would happen."[45]

But Emma was expecting a baby, and until it could be determined what she should do, she needed security and peace. She moved into the old homestead that had been her first home in Nauvoo, and rented the Mansion House to be run as a hotel, by William Marks. She gave birth to a little son, November 17, and in accordance with Joseph's wish concerning the child, she named him David Hyrum.

When the mantle of the prophet fell on Brigham Young, hundreds saw it, but Emma was not present. He took the leadership of the Church as President of the Twelve Apostles. One of his first official acts was to ask Emma to give up papers and deeds she had which he felt belonged to the Church. She refused. Further, since Brigham was absent from the city when Joseph was buried secretly in an unmarked grave, he could not appreciate Emma's refusal to allow him to place the bodies of Hyrum and Joseph in the tomb he had built near the temple, designated to be a final resting place for the Smith family. Because of the atmosphere of hate evidenced by the grim threats published abroad that "By next week there will not remain a Smith alive"— and knowledge that there was a price to be gained by anyone who could take Joseph's head back to Missouri, Emma kept the burial site a secret.

Her fears were not eased by the death of Joseph's younger brother, Samuel, July 30, just a month after the murder in Carthage took place. He had apparently sustained internal injuries during his mad ride, attempting to save his brothers. But Emma's confusion increased further due to the apostasy from the Church, a year after the martyrdom by her one remaining brother-in-law, William. While she did not support his claims to lead the church, his suspicious attitude toward Brigham Young and the other Church leaders served to unsettle Emma's sense of trust. William contended that Samuel was disposed of by ambitious parties who wished to seize control of the Church. His implication of Brigham Young was sufficient to cause the entire surviving members of Joseph's family to waver for a time.

William Smith was excommunicated from the Church for his rebellion against the leadership, and at October conference, (1845), President Young publically challenged Emma:

> We are determined also to use every means in our power to do all that Joseph told us. And we petition Sister Emma, in the name of Israel's God, to let us deposit the remains of Joseph, according as he commanded us. And if she will not consent to it, our garments are clean. Then when he awakens in the morning of the resurrection, he shall talk with them, not me. The sin be upon her head, not ours.[46]

The Apostles and Saints strove to assist and comfort Emma and her family after the martyrdom. President Young invited her to move west with the Saints. He said he would furnish conveyance for her and her children with provisions and means to take them to the mountains, but she refused to accept the offer. Fearing for Emma and her children's lives in those turbulent months before the exodus, Brigham Young set up a protective force around her home. Many years later her son indicated that the family believed they were under surveillance, and they resented what to them seemed an imposition on their privacy. One morning Emma discovered that a fire had been ignited in a pile of rubbish near the north wall of the Mansion during the night, scorching the paint on the boards but doing no worse damage. Emma believed this was an attempt to force her to go west. She attributed their safety to her having the manuscript of Joseph's Inspired Translation of the Bible, in the house. She felt Joseph had made her guardian of that document and refused to let the Church leaders have it.

All efforts failed to get her to change her mind and go west. Wilford Woodruff was one of her special friends who stopped to say goodbye. Emma gave him a scrap of oak left over from the construction of Joseph's coffin, for a walking staff. She also presented him a pair of white chiffon gloves and a handkerchief for his wife, Pheobe.

It was a sad day when Mary Fielding Smith and family came to the Mansion House and bid Mother Smith, Emma and family goodbye. Mary's daughter Martha Ann, who was five, later recalled how tears were shed and how Aunt Emma was deeply touched.

In December 1845, the first temple ordinances were performed in the almost completed temple, but Emma did not attend. When, in February, the first wagons crossed the frozen Mississippi for the western prairie, and an unsure western destination, Emma watched with sorrow, but with a firm conviction that they were all taking unnecessary risks. Emma had crossed that river on the ice two times, with small children. She did not see how she or anyone else should be called to do it again. A granddaughter wrote of this parting:

> Back in that deserted city, near the water's edge, stood the Mansion House, not long since completed, home of a tall, dark haired widow and her five children; an arrogant little beauty of fifteen, the adopted daughter Julia; a solemn brown eyed boy of nearly fourteen, Joseph; Frederick, past ten, merry and sunny, with the brown eyes of his mother; a lad of blue eyes like his father, Alexander; and the little brother, baby David,

loved and loving of them all, who was not quite two, for he was born after the cruel death of his father. [47]

When mobs threatened their safety, in the fall of 1846, Emma moved her household to a small apartment in Fulton, eight days travel from Nauvoo. They stayed until word came to Emma that her renter in the Mansion House was planning to leave and take Emma's furniture with him. She faced this new threat with the observation, "I have no friend but God and no place to go but home." And so she moved her children back into the Mansion House.

Time offers a tonic for the worst ills and sorrows which beset the human heart. Within three years after the martyrdom, Emma had won the love of Major Lewis C. Bidamon, whom she married in December 1847. Though the major had little schooling and had but a passing interest in the literature or religion which had absorbed Joseph, Emma seemed contented with her second companion.

Bidamon became the affable and generous landlord in the twenty- two room hotel, the Mansion house. He was a skilled workman in leather, wood, and metal. They had the farm near the city where the boys worked. With his help she reared her four sons to manhood, giving them what opportunities for education their limited resources permitted. After the exodus of the Saints, Emma's fortune in houses and land shrunk to a mere farthing. With everyone gone from Nauvoo the Hotel trade was very much diminished. The farm, her houses and lots would not represent the fortune some in Utah believed she had. She was forced to meet legal litigation to obtain title to her home and paid for her property several times over before this was accomplished.

Emma was bitter about the unkind attitude toward her by Brigham Young and other people in Utah, and she felt they would go to any lengths to do her harm.

Living quietly in the town which soon filled up with new citizens who knew little of the past, Emma tried to forget the turbulence and grief of her former life. She and Major Bidamon cared for Joseph's aged mother, Lucy, until her death in 1856. They were well loved by the children who lived in the community. Emma opened her arms and home to many orphans through the years, including the Major's two daughters, and a little son, Charlie Bidamon who came to her at the age of six; she loved him as her own son.

Emma lived 35 years after Joseph died. She is reported to have seldom spoken of religion, or of the Saints who had gone west. She taught her children to pray, to be honest and respect hard work, but she did not teach them the fullness of the gospel restored by her prophet-husband. She taught them that their father was a "good man." She saw her four sons married. But her trials were not over. Frederick died suddenly of pneumonia in 1862, and David Hyrum became gravely ill from some incurable condition that affected his mind. He was committed to the asylum at Elgin, Illinois. Emma referred to this as a "living sorrow," he died there in 1904, thirty years after his mother's death. Notwithstanding these sorrows added to those she had already endured, Emma found great joy in her grandchildren, and was a great influence in their lives.

Emma's oldest son, Joseph III became head of the "Reorganization" and devoted his entire life to debunking any idea that his father might have introduced the principle of plural marriage. His avid display of temper concerning this subject gave rise to public debates which carried forward into the next century. Though Emma was never excommunicated from the Church, she was labeled by the early leaders as an apostate, and a wicked woman because she allowed her sons to lead the Reorganization.

Though she was disdainful of the leaders in Utah, there is evidence that she still cherished in her heart the principles of the church her husband founded. In February, 1879, when questioned about her early experiences, Emma told her sons, "I know Mormonism to be the truth; and believe the church to have been established by divine direction." She also testified that he was a true prophet of God. This was only three months before she died.

In her patriarchal blessing given in 1833, Emma was told, "Thou shalt see many days, yea, the Lord will spare thee until thou art satisfied, for thou shalt see thy Redeemer. Thy heart shalt rejoice in the great work of the Lord, and no one shall take thy rejoicing from thee."[56]

As she suffered her last sickness, Emma was attended by Lewis Bidamon, Julia, and a friend, Sister Revel. Alexander arrived and, seeing her condition, telegraphed to Joseph III to come as quickly as he could. In the pre-dawn of 30 April 1879, Alexander was with her, and when she stretched out her left hand and said "Joseph, Joseph!" Alexander sprang to her side to hold her up, at the same time calling to his brother, "Joseph, Mother wants you." Joseph hurried to her, and the two sons watched as their mother sank back upon the pillow, let her arm fall, and quietly she breathed her last.[48]

The boys were remarking on her calling "Joseph, Joseph," and Sister Revel told them that a few days before, Emma had related to her a dream or vision. She told them Emma said Joseph came to her and took her into a beautiful mansion. As they passed through the apartments she saw an infant in a cradle whom she recognized as her baby, Don Carlos, who died in 1841. With great excitement she clasped the baby to her bosom and asked, "Joseph! Where are the rest of my children?" He replied, "Be patient, Emma, and you shall have all of your children."[49]

Alexander told this story in a talk he gave in 1906, testifying of the divinity of the Savior and the reality of resurrection and the doctrine of the celestial kingdom being a place where he hoped families would be together forever, living on this glorified, celestialized earth. In telling this story, Alexander said Sister Revel told him Emma saw "a personage of light, even the Lord Jesus Christ," standing beside Joseph.[50]

Her granddaughter paid Emma this tribute:

> Thus she lived, moved graciously, courageously, and consistently in her sphere of action, beloved by all who knew her best, writing her earth record with a firm unfaltering hand upon the tablet of the years, and when the sand had run their long course out, and the glass turned by a wise Creator towards a newer, fuller hour, quietly she gathered her robe about her in the calm repose of death, and went fearlessly forth to meet her Maker, upon her lips a last tribute and testimony to the character and virtue of the man she loved so well.[51]

It would appear from Alexander's testimony of his mother's vision, or dream, that at the end of her life, Emma left to her posterity her testimony of the principles she had apparently either forgotten or deliberately denied in the years of confusion into which she was placed after Joseph's death. She made grave mistakes at that time, which resulted in sad consequences for her posterity. But how basic in the gospel of Jesus Christ is the doctrine of the atonement. Since the Prophet and the Savior came to her to receive her at the end of her life, who are we to judge her?

Emma was an elect lady in the Church, fulfilling an essential calling as wife of the Prophet Joseph Smith. Notwithstanding her weakness, she was his companion in making sacred ordinances available to the Church in our day. She never denied her testimony of the divine origin of the Book of Mormon and that her husband Joseph was all he said he was, a Prophet of the living God. "If God raised up a Joseph as a prophet and a restorer of the Gospel truth . . . then he raised up an Emma as a helpmeet for him."[52]

Notes

[1] Lucy Mack Smith, *History of Joseph Smith*, Salt Lake City: Stevens & Wallis Inc., 1945), pp. 190-91.

[2] Joseph Smith, , B. H. Roberts, ed., 2nd ed. rev. (Salt Lake City: Deseret Book, 1978), 4:110. Hereafter cited as HC.

[3] HC 5:107.

[4] Raymond T. Bailey, "Emma Hale—Wife of the Prophet Joseph Smith" (Master's thesis, University, date), p. 8.

[5] Bailey, p. 8.

[6] Gracia N. Jones, *Emma's Glory and Sacrifice* (Hurricane, Utah: Homestead Publishers and Distributors, 1987), Page 3.

[7] Keith and Ann Terry, *A Dramatic Biography of Emma Smith* (Santa Barbara: Butterfly Publishing Inc., 1979), p. 6.

[8] Smith, p. 93.

[9] HC 1:17.

[10] Jones, p. 5.

[11] Emily C. Blackman, (Philadelphia: Claxton, Remson & Haffelfinger, 1873), p. 103.

[12] *A New Witness for Christ in America*, Vol. 1 (Salt Lake: Utah Printing Co., 1960), pp. 195-96.

[13] Jones, p. 21

[14] Cecil B. McGavin, The Family of Joseph Smith (Salt Lake City: Bookcraft, 1963), pp. 130-31.

[15] HC 1:108.

[16] HC 3:193.

[17] Written November 12, 1838 - Richmond, Mo. Through courtesy of late President Israel A. Smith of the Reorganized Church of Jesus Christ of Latter-day Saints.

[18] Smith, p. 286.

[19] Jones, p. 91

[20] Jones, p. 92

[21] HC 5:168.

[22] Ivan J. Barrett, *Joseph Smith and the Restoration*, (Provo, Young House: Brigham Young University Press, 1982), p. 506.

[23] *Ibid.*, p. 507.

[24] HC 4:567.

25 HC 4:552-53

26 HC 5:459.

27 HC 6:165-66.

28 Bailey, p. 114.

29 Jones, p. 135

30 Jones, p. 135

31 Jones, p. 139

32 Jones, p. 140

33 Jones, pp. 139-40

34 *Times and Seasons* 6:33

35 Benjamin F. Johnson's letter to George S. Gibbs. Historical Library, Salt Lake City, Utah. Benjamin F. Johnson File, Church, 1903.

36 *Journal of Discourses*, 27 Vols. (Liverpool and London: LDS Book Sellers Depot, 1855-86), 13: 194.

37 Andrew F. Ehat, (unpublished Doctoral thesis, BYU): "Joseph Smith's Introduction of Temple Ordinances and the 1844 Mormon Succession Question," p. 91-92)

38 Jones, p. 143.

39 Jones, p. 145.

40 Jones, p. 145.

41 Jones, p. 150.

42 Church Archives, Msd 5135.

43 Jones, p. 158.

44 Jones, p. 159.

45 Jones, p. 163.

46 HC 7:422-23.

47 Inez Smith Davis, *The Story of the Church* , (Independence, Mo.: Herald Printing House, 1977), p. 219.

48 Alexander Hale history quoted in Jones.

49 *Zion's Ensign*, December 31, 1903, RLDS Archives, quoted in Keith and Ann Terry.

50 Alexander Hale history quoted in Jones.

51 Mary Audentia Smith, *Ancestry and Posterity of Joseph Smith and Emma Hale*, (Independence, Mo.: Herald Printing House), p. 78.

52 Jones, p. 178.

Jane Elizabeth Manning James:
Our Black Heroine

With the thousands of recent converts streaming into Nauvoo in the early 1840's, none were more solicitous than the exhausted penury group of nine black Saints who entered the city on the bend of the Mississippi in the fall of 1843. They were led by a young black woman, Jane Elizabeth Manning and had walked over 800 miles from Connecticut. Little did they know, however, that Nauvoo would be just a temporary stop. Their respite there would be interrupted when Jane, with the body of the Mormons, would be forced to flee Illinois. She would endure the vigors and hardships of pioneer life to become part of the first black community in Salt Lake Valley.

Of Jane Elizabeth Manning's formative years, little is known aside from her "Life Sketch." She was the daughter of Isaac and Eliza Manning, born at Wilton, Connecticut, nestled on the Norwalk River. The Manning family were free black people, not held in slavery. Due to the death of her father, six-year-old Jane was sent to reside in the household of Joseph Fitch, a prosperous white farmer of Wilton. She worked as a servant, receiving instruction in Christian conduct but little educational or vocational training. In later life, having learned to read but not to write, she dictated her correspondence, her friends acting as scribes.

At fourteen years of age, she joined the Presbyterian Church but was soon dissatisfied with its dogma. In her life sketch she noted, "To me there was something more I was looking for." Within eighteen months after Jane's affiliation with the Presbyterians, Elder Charles Wesley Wandell, a Mormon missionary, proselytized in Wilton. He received "great encouragement, doors being freely opened to them in many places."[1] Jane met him, heard his message of the Prophet Joseph Smith and the revelations he had received. He also told her of the principles of the Mormon faith and of the city beautiful on the Mississippi River in Illinois. She quickly converted and acquainted her relatives with the restored truth. A number of them also converted.

Three weeks after her baptism in the Norwalk River, she was kneeling in prayer when the gift of tongues came upon her. About that time she was given a vision of the Prophet Joseph Smith. She told her family, "I have seen the Prophet of God in a vision. We must go to Nauvoo and see him for real."

As many of the converts in southwestern Connecticut were anxious to travel to Nauvoo, Elder Wandell organized a large group in October 1843, including Jane and eight members of her family. They traveled down the Erie Canal to Buffalo, New York, having arranged to have their travel fares collected when they reached Columbus, Ohio. However, in Buffalo the officers in charge of the travel insisted on being paid and would not take the Mannings any further. So Jane and her family started on foot from Buffalo, walking a distance of eight hundred miles to Nauvoo. Their shoes wore out. Their feet blistered and bled.

Jane enjoined the family to unite in prayer to the Lord. "We asked God the Eternal Father to heal our feet and our prayers were answered, and our feet were healed."[2]

In Peoria, Illinois, the authorities threatened to thrust the Mannings into jail unless they could produce papers showing they were free. Jane couldn't understand this demand as they had never been slaves. After a gruelling investigation they were permitted to continue their walk to Nauvoo. They waded a river in water up to their necks and spent the night in an abandoned log cabin, wet, cold, frightened, and hungry. That was a luxury as most of their nights were spent in the open, even when the snow fell. The frost was as thick as snow under their bare feet, but the devoted Jane remembered the faith that sustained them when she said, "We went on our way rejoicing, singing hymns and thanking God for His infinite goodness and mercy to us, in blessing us as He had, protecting us from all harm, answering our prayers and healing our feet."[3] As they approached LaHarpe, Illinois, they prayed for a sick baby, and it was healed. It was an exhilarating experience as they approached Nauvoo.

Arriving in the beautiful city of Nauvoo, they asked directions from Orson Spencer to the Prophet Joseph Smith's residence and then walked down Main Street to the Mansion House on the corner of Water Street. The Manning family stood before the front door and Jane knocked. They were greeted warmly by Sister Emma who was expecting them; for Jane had sent her a letter. Emma, with outstretched arms, welcomed them with, "Walk in. Come in all of you!"

Joseph and Dr. John Bernhisel entered the room. Jane knew Joseph because of her vision. The Prophet sat in a chair near Jane and said, "You have been the head of this little band, haven't you?"

"Yes, sir," Jane replied.

"God bless you," said the Prophet Joseph. "Now I would like you to relate your travel experiences." And Jane related in detail their hardships and trials in walking almost a thousand miles to see him and to be with the Saints. Brother Joseph slapped Dr. Bernhisel on the

knee and said, "What do you think of that Doctor? Isn't
that a demonstration of faith?"

Bernhisel shook his head slowly as he replied, "Well,
I rather think they have shown great faith. If I'd had to
do it I should not have come for I would not have had
faith enough." Then turning to the Mannings the
Prophet pronounced a benediction, "God bless you. You
are among friends now, and you'll be well cared for."

They were invited to stay at the Mansion House
until other homes could be found for them. Jane and
her kin remained with the Prophet and Sister Emma for
a week; then all except Jane were settled and had
secured work. When Jane arrived in Nauvoo she had
only two articles of clothing to cover her body. She had
sent a trunk full of "beautiful clothes" by boat expecting
them to be in Nauvoo when she arrived, but in St. Louis
a thief stole the trunk. After finding all her clothes gone
she sat on the porch of the Mansion and cried. The
Prophet Joseph coming up the walk saw her and asked,
"Where's all the folks?"

Jane sobbingly answered, "Brother Joseph, they have
all got themselves places, but I ain't got any place to live."

The Prophet consoled her, "You have a home right
here if you want it. You mustn't cry. We dry up all tears
here."

Jane continued, "I've lost my trunk and all my
clothes."

At this point Emma came out on the porch and her
husband said, "Go down to the store and clothe her
up." Then the Prophet continued, "Here is a girl who
says she has no home, haven't you a home for her?"

Emma replied, "Why yes, if she wants one." Then
she asked Jane, "What can you do?"

And Jane replied, "I can wash, iron, cook, and do
house work."

Sister Emma told Jane she could start her work in
the morning. She remained a member of Joseph Smith's

household until shortly before his death in Carthage. While there she enjoyed the association of Joseph and Emma's family and visited often with the Prophet's mother, Lucy. She also became friends with other members of the household such as Sarah and Marie Lawrence, and Eliza and Emily Partridge.

The room assigned to Jane in the Mansion house was reached by passing through the room of Lucy Mack Smith, the Prophet's mother. One morning as she entered Mother Smith's room, she was greeted with, "Good morning." and "Bring me that bundle from the bureau and sit down on the chair by me." Jane did as she was told. Jane placed the bundle in the hands of the aged woman, who then handed it back to her and directed Jane, "Handle this bundle and then put it in the top drawer of my bureau and lock it up." This done Jane sat on a chair, and Mother Smith, who had before told Jane about her son Joseph's troubles and difficulties in translating and publishing the Book of Mormon, solemnly said, "Do you remember that I told you about the Urim and Thummim when I told you about the Book of Mormon?"

"Yes, Ma'am," replied Jane.

"You have just handled it within that bundle. You are not permitted to see it. You will live long after I am dead and gone, and you can tell the Latter-day Saints that you were permitted to handle the Urim and Thummim."

Sister Emma depended on Jane, who was a good, reliable worker, and was never disappointed in the quality of work she performed. One day when they were alone Emma asked Jane, "Would you like to be adopted to us as our child?" After reflecting for two weeks, Jane declined the offer. She had not been taught the principle of sealing and would not understand it until years to come. Later she recalled, "I did not understand or know what it meant. They were always good and kind to me but I did not know my own mind. I did not comprehend."[4]

Having lived with the Smith family, Jane was asked in later years to describe the Prophet Joseph. She said he treated her as one of his own children. Every time he saw her he would greet her with, "God bless you," and pat her on the shoulder. He was tall, over six feet; he was a fine, big, noble, beautiful man! He had blue eyes and light hair, and very fine white skin. She personally knew his kindness and generosity. The desolation she felt at his death was poignantly expressed:

"When he was killed, I liked to a died myself. If it had not been for the teachers, I felt so bad, and the teachers told me, 'You can't want to die because he did. He died for us and now we want to live and do all the good we can.'"[5] However, in the years that followed she recalled, "I shall never forget the agony and sorrow."

Some time after the martyrdom of the Prophet and Patriarch she was invited by President Brigham Young to live with his family. While she was living with the President of the Quorum of Twelve Apostles she married Isaac James, a free black who was born in the rural Marmouth County, New Jersey. He was converted to Mormonism at age nineteen and had migrated to Nauvoo. In the spring of 1846, she and Isaac left Nauvoo to accompany President Brigham Young to the Rocky Mountains. Passing through the territory of Iowa they, with other Saints, crossed the Missouri River and stayed the winter at Winter Quarters, a temporary pioneer camp. There Jane gave birth to their son, Silas.

In mid-June, following the departure of the pioneers under President Brigham Young and his counselors Heber C. Kimball and Willard Richards, the main company of pioneers trekking west, who numbered 1500 souls, started their journey. Black faces turned resolutely toward the west; Jane and Isaac James and their, son Silas, were counted in the lead company of the main encampment numbered in the second fifty of the first hundred. Ira Eldredge was their captain.

The company encountered hardships in crossing the plains and the mountains. Forage often was inadequate, weakening the oxen who were already fighting fatigue. At times suitable fords for crossing rivers were difficult to locate. Blinding dust storms obliterated their vision. Herds of buffalo, though a source of fresh meat, often passed dangerously close to the wagon train and once stampeded the livestock. When the company reached the Green River on 5 September, Captain Eldredge dispatched his vanguard company, which included the James family, to proceed as quickly as possible to the Salt Lake Valley to request reinforcements. They entered the uninviting Salt Lake Valley 19 September 1847.

Jane and her family first camped on Temple Block until she and Isaac built a house in the center of the block north of the Temple Block. Then four years later, they moved a half mile east from Liberty Park. The first years of the Jameses in the Salt Lake Valley were marked with periods of poverty. Jane recalled in later years: "Oh, how I suffered of cold and hunger and keenest of all was to hear my little ones crying for bread, and I had none to give them, but in all the Lord was with us and gave us grace and faith to stand it all."

She at times walked down to get milk from Isaac Chase's wife, Elizabeth, when she had not a thing in the house to eat and her little children were crying from hunger. Yet still she felt much chagrined having to beg milk. Eventually the James family's hard work, thrift and perseverance helped them acquire a fine home, farm lands, and animals. Three horses replaced the ox, a new "vehicle" replaced their rickety old cart. Jane spun and wove cloth for her family's clothing. There was a time when "only four other households in the First Ward in Salt Lake City held more property than the Jameses." But just when they felt they could rejoice in the bounty, the grasshoppers and crickets came along carrying destruction wherever they went, laying our crops to the ground , bringing poverty and desolation throughout this beautiful valley."[7]

Jane Elizabeth Manning James' dictated biography is skimpy and sporadic, but what is there and available from other sources shed some light on qualities of her character. One of her most notable traits was generosity. She shared what little she had with her neighbors. When Apostle Amasa M. Lyman started on a mission to California with Orrin Porter Rockwell, leaving his wife and children destitute, Eliza Lyman noted in her journal, "We baked the last of our flour today, and have no prospect of getting more till after harvest. . . . Not long after Amasa was gone, Jane James, the colored woman, let me have two pounds of flour, it being half of what she had."[8]

Jane, who was faithfully active in the Eighth Ward Relief Society, contributed of her sparse means to special projects, and donated toward the construction of the St. George, Logan, and Manti temples. She contributed toward such other Church causes as the Lamanite (Indian) Mission, the Deseret Hospital, and a People's Party banner during a bitterly contested campaign in 1890. In recognition of her services and limited income, the Relief Society regularly sent her a Christmas basket filled with packages of meat, dried fruit, sugar, and other needed staples.

In recognition of her service extended beyond the boundaries of her ward, Church authorities, at conference time, regularly reserved seats in the center front of the tabernacle for our black Saint Jane.

Another admirable feature of her character was her poise and dignity, maintained despite her personal and financial adversity. She took pride in her personal appearance. Underlying her dignity was a reservoir of endurance in times of adversity. She was ever active in her faith. She was an unwavering member of the Relief Society. She helped with special projects. Her undaunted faith was combined with her loving generosity to her family and church. Throughout her life Jane James asserted her iden-

tity as both a black and a Mormon and retained her sense
of personal worth and dignity. The difficulties she had in
life never changed her open committments to the gospel.
She was true and black to the end.[9]

A distressing, sorrowful test of faith for Jane was
recurring death in her family. She was the mother of ten
children, and she outlived all but two of them. Of her
seven children who reached maturity, five died before
the age of forty. Two of her daughters died in childbirth. A third daughter moved to California in her early
twenties, married a Methodist minister and with him
served for six years as a missionary in Liberia before
dying at age thirty-eight. Mortality statistics were grim
among Jane's grandchildren. Of fourteen, six died
before reaching the age of four. Often as she mused
upon the losses of her dear children and grandchildren,
she smilingly recalled in poetic frame:

> Tell me the old, old story
> Sang Mary Ann to me,
> As the dancing feet of the little maid
> Sprang lightly to my knee.
>
> And again the childish voices
> Of the far off long ago,
> Seem to echo the simple sweet refrain
> Across the drifting snow—
>
> Tell me the old, old story
> Tell me the old, old story
> Tell me the old, old story
> Of Jesus and His love—

And then looking heavenward she sighed, "They
now know of Jesus and His love. The Lord giveth and
the Lord taketh away, blessed be the name of the Lord.
But I spun all the cloth for my family for years."

Another disaster awaited Jane. Her husband, Isaac
James, left her and the children in 1869. He sold his share
of the property to our black heroine for $500. During the

twenty-year separation she managed her home and raised her family. She always had vegetables from her garden. She was adept at spinning, sewing and soap-making which provided them with other necessities. From her work as a laundress a meager cash income was acquired. She moved her family into a two-story frame house with a white picket fence enclosing it. Her son, Sylvester, became a member of the Nauvoo Legion in Utah. The children helped with the sheep. The coming of grandchildren, children, relatives and friends did much to compensate for the absence of material possessions.

Finally at the close of twenty years, Isaac returned to Jane and the children then living. He reestablished his relationship with both his wife and the Church. But he really came home to die, for less than two years after his arrival he died and Jane held his funeral in her home in 1891. At this time it was not unusual for funerals to be held in a home.[10]

Racial practices were a test of "Aunt Jane's" faith as her letters to the presiding authorities attest. Although a member of the Mormon faith, Jane remained racially conscious. She had lived in the Mansion House when the Prophet was a candidate for President of the United States and she seemed to hear, as though it were yesterday, the Prophet Joseph saying, "Break off the shackles from the poor black man, and hire him to labor like other human beings, for an hour of virtuous liberty on earth is worth an eternity of bondage."[11]

Jane revered Joseph Smith and, late in life, referred to him as "the finest man I ever saw on earth." She noted significantly, "Things came to pass what he prophesied about the colored race being free. Things that he told has come to pass. I did not hear that, but I knew of it."[12]

Jane was able to perceive the millennial expectation of peace during the reign of Christ combined with her future eternal salvation. She understood the importance of the endowment and supplicated the prophets many times for temple blessings.

President Brigham Young taught the Saints, "Your endowment is to receive all the ordinances in the House of the Lord which are necessary for you, after you have departed this life, to enable you to walk back to the presence of the Father, passing the angels who stand as sentinels, being enabled to give them the key words, the signs and tokens, pertaining to the Holy Priesthood and gain your eternal exaltation in spite of earth and hell."[13] In a letter to President John Taylor on 27 December 1884, she wrote:

> I realize my race and color and can't expect my endowments as others who are white. My race was handed down through the flood and God promised Abraham that in his seed all the nations of the earth should be blest and as this is the fullness of all dispensations is there not a blessing for me?
>
> I am the only one of my father's family that kept the faith. You know my history and according to the best of my ability I have lived to all the requirements of the Gospel. Living with Brother Joseph and family Sister Emma came to me and asked me how I would like to be adopted to them as a child. I did not comprehend it and she came again. I was so green I did not give her a decided answer and Joseph died. If I could be adopted to him as a child my soul would be satisfied.[14]

Jane appealed to President Taylor to lay her case before his counselors George Q. Cannon and Joseph F. Smith in being adopted to Brother Joseph. A recommend was given her, signed by her stake president, Angus M. Cannon, to enter the temple and be baptized for her dead kindred. She was told to be content with this privilege. Nevertheless, she was untiringly persistent. We have noted that her husband deserted her, although he had worked for President Brigham Young as his coachman. As a conscientious Mormon, marriage to her was indispensable for her eternal salvation and must be solemnized in the temple to extend beyond the grave through eternity. She wrote Joseph F. Smith, counselor in the First Presidency, and requested to be sealed to another man whom she felt was more worthy to spend eternal life with her.

In that letter she appealed again for her endowment and to be adopted into Brother Joseph Smith the Prophet's family. Her appeal was considered by President Wilford Woodruff who presented it to his counselors and the Quorum of Twelve Apostles. He referred to her as "a negress of long standing in the Church." The minutes of the meeting state that her appeal could not be granted. Her final appeal was made to Joseph F. Smith after he was sustained Prophet and President of the Church, and she enclosed a stamped envelope for his reply. Sadly, his answer too had to be no, and Jane resolved to wait until she met her Lord and make her appeal to Him. [Temple work—endowments and sealings—has recently been done for Jane and her family.][15]

She lived her last days with the hope that revelation would provide the black Saints with all the blessings in the temple. Had she lived three quarters of a century later, her hope would have been realized when President Spencer W. Kimball received that revelation extending temple blessings to all worthy males and of course this took in females of the black race as well. (D&C Official Declaration —2)

Jane remained a steadfast member of the Church of Jesus Christ of Latter-day Saints throughout a life filled with sorrows, trials, and severe reverses. Her life did not bring historical recognition or wide acclaim. Today, nearly eighty-five years after her death, not even a stone marks her resting place in the Salt Lake City Cemetery. Her achievements were selfless yet personal.

Jane Elizabeth Manning James closed her life sketch

in her old age of nearly ninety years. She was partially blind, which was a great trial to her, but hoped her sight would be spared "to me poor as it is that I may be able to go to meeting and to go to the temple to do my work for my dead. My faith in the Gospel of Jesus Christ of Latter-day Saints, is as strong today, nay, it is if possible stronger than it was the day I was first baptized. I pay my tithes and offerings, keep the word of wisdom, I go to bed early and rise early. I try in my feeble way to set a good example to all."[16]

Jane was loved and respected by the Saints in the Mormon community. President Joseph F. Smith spoke at her funeral services held in the Eighth Ward chapel. The chapel was crowded, many in the congregation being of her own race. The Deseret News noted: "Flowers in profusion were contributed by friends who had learned to respect and love the deceased for her undaunted faith and goodness of heart."[17]

Notes

[1] Henry J. Wolfinger, "Life Sketch," in *A Test of Faith*, unpublished manuscript, Washington D. C., 1954.

[2] *Ibid.*, p. 19.

[3] Wolfinger, p. 20.

[4] *Ibid.*, p. 20.

[5] Wolfinger, p. 21.

[7] Joseph Smith, *History of the Church*, Vol. 6, p. 205.

[8] "Biography of Jane Elizabeth Manning James," dictated by Jane in later life. Early parts of it found in Young Woman's Journal, Vol. 16, covering January 1905 to December 1905. Salt Lake City, Deseret News, pp. 551-553.

[9] Kate B. Carter, *The Negro Pioneer* (Salt Lake City: Utah Printing Co., 1965), pp. 9-10.

[10] Linda King Newell and Valeen Tippets Avery, "Jane Manning James, Black Saint, 1847 Pioneer. *Ensign*, August 1979, pp. 26-29.

[11] "Joseph Smith the Prophet," Young Woman's Journal, Vol. 16, No. 12, December 1905. Deseret News, Salt Lake City, p. 553.

[12] HC, Vol. 6, p. 203.

[13] Young Woman's Journal, op cit, p. 553.

[14] *Journal of Discourses* 27 vols. (Liverpool and London: LDS Book Sellers, 1855-86), 2:31.

[15] Wolfinger, p. 17.

[16] Newell and Avery, p. 29.

[17] Wolfinger.

[18] Quoted in Wolfinger, p. 12.

Eliza Roxey Snow:
Zion's Poetess

Eliza R. Snow was the most prominent, the most il-
lustrious, and the best known Mormon woman of her
time. She was the sister of the scholarly Lorenzo Snow
who, in his eighty-fourth year, became the President of
the Church. She was also one of the plural wives of the
Prophet Joseph Smith, being sealed to him on 29 June
1842.

Few women have been as gifted and as richly
endowed with poetic ability as she. She was an original
thinker and talented not only as a writer but also as a
speaker. She was dignified, ladylike, ever composed;
she was never fussy, yet always busy. She possessed to
a high degree "the striking energy of character, tenacity
of purpose" and perseverance that characterized the
heroic mothers of New England—even back to the
Mayflower days—from whom she was descended.[1]
Referring to her ancestry she once wrote: "Our Father
was a native of Massachusetts, our Mother of
Connecticut, and were descendants of the genuine
Puritan stock—those who fled from religious persecution in the 'old world', and landed on Plymouth Rock,
of historic celebrity."[2]

With Eliza R. Snow, industry and economy went hand in hand throughout her life. She was a severe disciplinarian—especially with herself. She was ever punctual, orderly, and particular. She possessed remarkable powers of concentration; and this, combined with her excellent ability and blended with almost perfect control, gave her resoluteness of character in the highest degree.

Besides her literary talents, she had strong abilities as a leader and as an organizer. Justice was one of her strong points; and though she, like Portia, believed that "the quality of mercy is not strained," yet she often said, "Justice before mercy."

She was skilled in household accomplishments such as sewing and needlework, "but she possessed a literary talent which was destined to eclipse all commonplace acquirements."[3] With all this God-given talent she believed, as did Lord Byron, that a poet should do something more than write verses. She practiced what she wrote in beautiful, easy-flowing poetry. She labored incessantly for the building up of the Kingdom of God, especially as a teacher and counselor to the women of the Church.[4] The appreciative Saints gave her the title of "Zion's Poetess,"[5] a name to her of far greater worth than all the high-sounding titles and praises which the world could possibly bestow upon her.

This remarkable woman was born in Becket, Berkshire County, Massachusetts on 21 January 1804, the second daughter of Oliver and Rosetta Snow. As early as 1806, her parents moved to Mantua, Portage County, Ohio. Here five more children were born, two daughters and three sons. The eldest of these three boys was Lorenzo who was ten years Eliza's junior. Lorenzo and Eliza were very fond of one another. Seldom does one find such a sweet, considerate, and close brother-sister relationship.

As a young man, Lorenzo had an insatiable urge to learn. Eliza tells us that the common answer to the inquiry from his associates as to his whereabouts was, "Hid up with his book." But although he was trained from infancy in religion, Lorenzo had devoted little or no personal attention or study to the subject.

When Lorenzo was twenty-one, Eliza made him a suit of clothes of which he was very fond. He called this suit his "freedom suit"[6] because it was given to him on his twenty-first birthday. As a young man, his ambition strongly led him in the direction of a military career. Step by step he gained military promotion. His sister Eliza feared, however, that this military road would eventually lead him to the battlefield and her heart ached as she anticipated the outcome. She frequently entreated him to drop his plans for the military; but all her persuasion was in vain. It must have been a great sacrifice for her to grant his request to sew his uniform, but she did and lovingly describes it as being "beautiful, magnificent . . . and my brother took as much pride, if not of military pride, of self-satisfaction as ever Napoleon won a battle."[7] Fortunately, his military career was of short duration. He felt he could not satisfy his ambition without a college education.

The Snows were Baptists by religion, but they were liberal to people of all denominations and broad-minded in their thinking. Their home was the very essence of hospitality and was a "resort for intelligent and exemplary spirits."[8] In Eliza's girlhood she became acquainted with such leading spirits in the field of religious reform as Alexander Campbell, a noted scholar, theologian, and founder of the "Disciples" Church. He and his co-laborers in reform, namely Walter Scott and Sidney Rigdon, were frequent visitors at her father's home. These men of learning took pains to assist Eliza in the study of the Bible, especially with the Old Testament prophets. It is reasonable to assume that her scriptural studies under their guidance aided in preparing her mind to receive the gospel in its fullness.

Eliza's father was a farmer, but he also devoted much of his time to public business; and he was in need of a secretary to assist him. Who was better qualified for this service than Eliza? It was "a species of employment for which her natural capacities rendered her well adapted."[9]

She entered upon her literary career when quite young, winning praise and recognition as a young poetess with great potential. She had become so well-known for her literary accomplishments that when, on Independence Day of 1826, John Adams and Thomas Jefferson died simultaneously, she was urgently solicited through the press to write a requiem for them. With the appearance of the poem, the young poetess found herself becoming famous. But the prospect of a successful and perhaps brilliant literary career was sacrificed "upon the altar of her religious convictions."[10]

Along with her poetic nature she "possessed a profound and exalted spiritual temperament."[11] The sublime and soul-satisfying poetry of the Bible was her delight. She loved the scriptures and read them daily. One of the most powerful attributes of her gentle nature was a sublime reverence for God. Her feelings of reverence for God and of man's close relationship with his Heavenly Father is beautifully expressed in her "Invocation, or the Eternal Father and Mother," written in 1843. This inspiring poem was penned by Eliza at Nauvoo and soon became the most widely sung hymn in the Church. The profound doctrine "I've a mother there" was given to her by revelation from her contact with the Prophet Joseph Smith. Intense love for the gospel and interest in the women's part led to many deep and earnest thoughts about the doctrine of salvation. The new light that the restored gospel turned on marriage and motherhood glorified woman. What was her place in the eternal scheme of God's plan? Would she, Eliza, know her mother in the future life? Taking these soul-stirring questions to the Prophet, she received from him the light and inspiration which resulted in her writing of the hymn later entitled "O My Father."[12]

> O my Father, Thou that dwellest,
> In the high and glorious place!
> When shall I regain thy presence,
> And again behold thy face?
> In thy holy habitation,
> Did my spirit once reside;
> In my first primeval childhood,
> Was I nurtured near thy side?
> In the heavens are parents single?
> No, the thought makes reason stare:
> Truth is reason, truth eternal,
> Tells me I've a mother there.
> When I leave this frail existence—
> When I leave this mortal by:
> Father, Mother, may I meet you
> In your royal court on high?

This poem alone has immortalized Eliza R. Snow. Orson F. Whitney has written, "If all her other writings, prose and verse were swept into oblivion, this poem alone, the sweetest and sublimest of all the songs of Zion, would perpetuate her fame and render her name immortal."[13]

There is an anecdote well-known among members of the Church during the last two decades of the nineteenth century:

It is said that the celebrated Evangelist of America, Theodore Parker, had in his service a Mormon woman; that he had known nothing of her connection with the Mormon Church; that this female disciple of the Mormon Prophet, in a spirit of praiseworthy cunning to captivate her Master's mind with the striking conceptions of her church on the subject of pre-existence, placed a little book of Eliza R. Snow's poems near his hand; that Theodore Parker read the hymn "O My Father," was captivated with its conceptions of our

Father and Mother God and their courts on high; that
he talked to his servant of this hymn and the Mormons;
and that Eliza R. Snow's hymn gave the inspiration to
the unique form of invocation "to our Father and
Mother God" which characterized Theodore Parker's
adorations and prayers.[14]

In the autumn of 1820, the tidings of the young
Joseph Smith's first vision of the Father and the Son
reached the ears of Eliza, living with her parents in
Mantua, Ohio. Was it true, she mused, that God had
raised up a prophet in her day, and was about to restore
the gospel with all "its gifts and powers?" She wrote: "I
heard of Joseph Smith as a prophet, to whom the Lord
was speaking from the heavens; and that a sacred
record containing the history of the origin of the aborig-
ines of America was unearthed."

She pondered considerably all she heard. "Could it
possibly be true? I considered it a hoax—too good to be
true."

Then in January 1832 the Prophet Joseph visited the
Snow family in Mantua. Eliza was fascinated with the
Prophet and his beliefs, but was cautious. She scruti-
nized his face as closely as she could without attracting
his attention and "decided that his was an honest face."
At her father's home that evening, "the most impressive
testimonies I had ever heard were given by two of the
witnesses of the Book of Mormon. To hear men testify
that they had seen an angel—that they had listened to
his voice bearing testimony of the work that was usher-
ing in a new dispensation, thrilled my utmost soul."[15]

Impressed though Eliza may have been, she waited
three more years, until 1835, before committing herself
to baptism.

Early in the year 1835, Eliza's mother and her elder
sister Leonora, having previously joined the Church,
visited the Saints in Kirtland. Upon their return to
Mantua, their testimonies were so strong, beautiful, and

convincing that Eliza began to fear that the news of the restoration of the gospel by the Prophet Joseph Smith was too joyful to be true. However, she pursued her investigations for a short time with increasing faith, until she found that all her mother and sister had told her was true; then, on 5 April 1835, she was baptized. She wrote, "The spirit bore testimony of the truth. I felt that I had waited already a little too long to see whether the work was going to 'flash in the pan' and go out. But my heart was now fixed."[16]

Hers was an extraordinary experience. That evening, after her baptism in a stream of water, she retired to bed "reflecting on the wonderful events transpiring around me, I felt an indescribable, tangible sensation commencing at my head and enveloping my person and passing off at my feet, producing inexpressible happiness. Immediately following, I saw a beautiful candle with an unusual long, bright blaze directly over my feet," she joyously recalled.

The interpretation was given her of the vision of the candle and flame above her feet: "The light of intelligence shall be lighted over your path. I was satisfied."[17]

In the autumn of 1835, Eliza bade farewell to her home, to the fond associations of her youth, and to the flattering prospects of becoming a celebrated poetess. She was fully determined to unite forever with the evilly-spoken-of and much-persecuted Saints. In a poem called "Evening Thoughts or What It Means To Be a Saint," she describes her firm resolve:

> My heart is fixed—I know in whom I trust.
> 'Twas not for wealth—'twas not to gather heaps
> Of perishable things—'twas not to twine
> Around my brow a transitory wreath,
> A garland deck'd with gems of mortal praise,
> That I forsook the home of childhood; that
> I left the lap of ease—the halo rife
> With friendship's richest, soft, and mellow tones;

Affection's fond caresses, and the cup
O'er flowing with the sweets of social life,
With high refinement's golden pearls enrich'd.
Ah, no! a holier purpose fired my soul;
A nobler object prompted my pursuit.
Eternal prospects open'd to my view,
And hope celestial in my bosom glow'd.

God, who commanded Abraham to leave
His native country, and to offer up
On the lone altar, where no eye beheld
But that which never sleeps, an only son,
Is still the same; and thousands who have made
A covenant with Him to sacrifice,
Are bearing witness to the sacred truth—
Jehovah speaking has revealed His will.

* * *

But yet, although to be a Saint requires
A noble sacrifice—an arduous toil—
A persevering aim; the great reward
Awaiting the grand consummation will
Repay the price, however costly; and
The pathway of the Saint the safest path
Will prove; though perilous;

* * *

Then let me be a Saint, and be prepar'd
For the approaching day.[18]

And Sister Eliza lived the life of a Saint, ever helpful
to those in need, ever lending cheer to those downcast,
ever comforting those who were in need of comfort, and
ever ready and anxious to impart of her knowledge and
substance toward the building of the kingdom.

After her arrival in Kirtland she boarded with the
family of the Prophet Joseph Smith. She taught a school
in Kirtland which was referred to as a "select school for
young ladies." It was also said to be the "Prophet's family school." One of her biographers suggests, "She was,

perhaps, the first woman school teacher in the Church."[19]

She, being a Saint in very deed, was determined to help with her means to build the Kirtland Temple. She tells us:

> Soon after my arrival, I sent for the "Building Committee of the Kirtland Temple," and on my asking them if they would like a little money, they replied that they had a payment to make soon, and did not know where the means was coming from. I do not recollect how much I gave them; however, it was sufficient to cover the present liability of the committee, who felt greatly relieved, and proposed to send me their note of hand for the amount. I told them that I did not want a note—they were welcome to the money; however, they sent the note, and some time after wished me to accept a house and lot—thus redeeming their note.[20]

The amount given the building committee by Eliza must have been considerable for the lot given her was a valuable one, situated near the temple. According to Heber C. Kimball, lots were selling in Kirtland at this time for five hundred dollars; and this lot was a choice one, being so near the House of the Lord then under construction. The value of the lot was greatly enhanced by fruit trees, an excellent spring of water, and a house which accommodated two families. Sister Eliza says, "it was truly an enviable situation," for although she was boarding with the Prophet while teaching his family school, her older, widowed sister wanted a home in Kirtland. So Eliza let Leonora live in part of the house and rented the other part. She was convinced that the "hand of God was too plainly visible" in this ever to "be mistaken."[21]

While in Kirtland, Eliza's life and labors were concentrated and centered upon that which, through the gospel plan, would bring salvation to some erring soul.

In her poetic expressions "no other theme could ever
again inspire her muse."

"In several of her poems, written at this early period
of her experience in the Church, is shown how entirely
she had withdrawn herself from the allurements of
worldly ambition."[22] In a poem entitled "Two Chapters
of the Life of President Joseph Smith," she wrote:

> For thy approval, Lord, shall prompt my pen,
> Regardless of the praise or blame of men.
>
> * * *
>
> Thy approbation is the boon, I claim;
> With that, it matters not who praise or blame.[23]

One of the biggest spiritual thrills to come to Sister
Eliza during her sojourn in Kirtland occurred when her
beloved young brother Lorenzo came into the Church.
He had been a young man who didn't appear to be
much inclined towards religion. After a brief time at the
Presbyterian College at Oberlin, he wrote his sister, "If
there is nothing better than is to be found here in
Oberlin College, goodbye to all religions."[24]

However, Eliza was ever patient and hopeful. She
answered his questions, and, knowing that he was interested in crowning his collegiate studies with a mastery of
Hebrew, invited him to Kirtland following his first year at
Oberlin, where he had studied under Professor Seixas.
Lorenzo responded to her invitation and went to Kirtland,
without the slightest idea of embracing Mormonism. Yet
while he studied Hebrew with such men as the Prophet
Joseph, Newel K. Whitney, and other Saints, "his mind
also drank in, and his heart became imbued with the living faith of the everlasting gospel. . . . and not many weeks
passed after his arrival, before he was baptized into the
Church of Jesus Christ of Latter-day Saints."[25]

And what a marvelous change came over young
Lorenzo by this one act of stepping into the waters of

baptism and receiving the Holy Ghost by the laying on of hands. A new world was opened to him. He seemed to be invested with a sixth sense—"the sense which comprehends the things of God."[26]

His sister rejoiced over this change:

> How wonderfully changed all his youthful aims! How suddenly they sink into insignificance! How extended the sphere of his youthful anticipations! How glorious—how exalted the motive power, the incentive which now prompts his youthful ambition. Instead of earthly military renown, he now enters the area for championship with the armies of heaven—the achievements of the Gods, crowned with the laurels of eternity, everlasting glory, honor and eternal lives.[27]

And for the rest of his mortal life, these chaste and selfless motives prompted his actions and governed his entire existence. He became the President of the Church, and, during a brief three-year administration, rejuvenated the membership in their financial obligation to the Kingdom of God and lent emphasis to the world-wide mission of the Church, that every nation and people might be privileged to hear the "glad tidings" of the restoration.

His saintly life was reflected in his very countenance. The Reverend Dr. Prentis, who met Lorenzo Snow in the year 1898 when Lorenzo was 84 years of age, wrote: "For a second I was startled to see the holiest face but one I had ever been privileged to look upon. His face was a power of peace; his presence a benediction of peace. In the tranquil depths of his eyes were not only the "house of silent prayer" but the abode of spiritual strength."[28]

Sister Eliza's father also embraced the faith, and soon she welcomed both her parents and her brothers and sisters to Kirtland.

Late in April 1838, Eliza left Kirtland with her father's family and a few other Saints for Far West, Missouri, reaching there on July 16. The poetess of Zion and all others going with her to Missouri were royally entertained the first night out from Kirtland by Charlotte Snow Granger, one of her father's sisters. Eliza mentions that if they had been a bridal party they could not have been treated with more respect and served more bounteously. This was surely unusual for those days. They were Mormons and Mrs. Granger was a popular Presbyterian, yet she was too noble-minded to be narrow and bigoted.[29]

About one hundred miles out from Far West, Lorenzo suffered a racking pain in his head which became steadily worse from the jolting of the wagon. Eliza cradled his head in her arms to relieve the excruciating suffering.

Upon their arrival in Far West they were met by Sidney Rigdon who insisted that Lorenzo be taken to his home. Eliza cared for her brother while her parents continued their journey to Adam-ondi-Ahman. While nursing Lorenzo back to health, she had difficulty with a persistent doctor, Dr. Sampson Avard, whose services were not helping her brother. Later, this doctor was associated with the infamous Danite band. Eliza had asked Dr. Avard for some medicine, but he insisted on going with her to see the patient. It seemed to Eliza afterward that Lorenzo's fever increased. Eliza was determined to get rid of Avard, tactfully asking him for his bill. He immediately sensed what she was getting at and angrily threatened that if he did not attend Lorenzo, he would surely not recover. However, when he found Eliza resolute in her determination, he yielded, presented his bill, and left in a huff.

Even the family of Sidney Rigdon seems to have had more faith in doctors than in God and blamed Eliza severely for discharging the doctor. They were so displeased with her that they seldom offered to assist her in the care of her brother, although they were kind enough to her. But her trust in God and her faith in the power of prayer plus her kind, sisterly nursing paid off; and within two weeks, Lorenzo was sufficiently recovered to resume his journey to Diahman.

As she looked upon the industry of the Saints gathered in the sacred valley of Adam-ondi-Ahman where the great patriarch of the human family had blessed his children three years before his death, the poetess of Zion could not withhold the inner emotions of her soul; and she burst into song:

> Awake! my slumbering Minstrel; thou has lain
> Like one that's numbered with the unheeded slain!
> Unlock thy music—let thy numbers flow
> Like torrents bursting from the melting snow.
>
> * * *
>
> To catch thy notes, and bear thy strains away
> To regions where celestial minstrels play;
> Because the theme which now inspires thy song
> Is one that interests the heavenly throng.
>
> The God who talked to Adam face to face
> Is speaking now, in these latter days,
> And all the righteous men that ever stood
> Unite their faith to roll the kingdom forth,
> Until the "Little Stone" shall fill the earth.[30]

Father Snow had purchased two homesteads at Adam-ondi-Ahman. Eliza states that the Missourians "were very anxious to sell, and were obsequiously kind towards the strangers who had come among them, and who did not suspect what the sequel showed, that arrangements had been made by many, prior to selling, to mob and drive the Saints and retake possession of the purchased premises."[31]

In the trouble which arose between the Saints and the Missourians, mobs occupied Diahman, and all the

Saints were forced to leave Daviess County within ten days. The Snow family was compelled to leave all that they had purchased, after being permitted to live upon it for less than one year. Even before the time allotted had expired, the former owner of the homesteads came. Looking around arrogantly and impudently, he demandingly blurted: "I'll claim possession of my now reclaimed land. How soon can you be out of the house?" Suppressing with a strong effort their indignation, they departed.

It was a bitterly cold winter day, and Eliza, after assisting her parents with the loading of the wagons, walked ahead of the teams in an effort to warm her freezing feet. As she walked along, a Missourian rode up and taunted her, "I think this will cure you of your faith."

Undaunted Eliza looked him squarely in the eyes and defiantly replied, "No sir, it will take more than this to cure me of my faith!"

Upon receiving such a courageous retort, the man's countenance fell; and, shrugging his shoulders, he went on his way with, "Well, I must confess you are a better soldier than I am." Eliza was not so sure that she could consider this remark a compliment, coming as it did from the lips of a man who, with others of his kind, had been responsible for driving them from their homes.

The Snows, along with the other exiled Saints, made their homes in Illinois—the majority of them the beautiful new city of Nauvoo. There Eliza taught school. During the trying days of the flight from Missouri, she had strengthened and edified the Saints through the inspiration which flowed from her pen as she was guided by the Holy Spirit. And, oh, how her people needed the help that she was endowed to give them!

At Nauvoo she wrote much, both in poetry and in prose, her main theme—and it was a thrilling one—being the recent persecution of her people. In her "Appeal to Americans," she penned:

There's a dark, foul stain on the Eagle's crest,
For Columbia's sons have her sons oppressed;
And chased into exile, now they roam
Far away from their land and their much loved
    home.

Awake! all ye sons of Freedom, awake,
And redeem your cause, for Columbia's sake.
Give us back our rights e're eternal shame
Shall wither the wreath of our country's fame.[32]

The Relief Society was organized on 17 March 1842 by the Prophet Joseph Smith, and Eliza was chosen as secretary. She continued in this capacity until the martyrdom, which temporarily dissolved the society. As its secretary, Eliza had the duty of seeing that the meetings opened and closed on time, but she had no timepiece. The Prophet, noting this, laid his own handsome gold watch on the table for her use, later presenting it to Eliza as a gift. She later gave that watch to President Joseph F. Smith, whose son, Joseph Fielding Smith, the tenth President of the Church received it from his father.[33]

As secretary of the Relief Society, Eliza wrote the petition proposed by Emma Smith, president of the society, asking protection from the governor of Illinois for her husband, the Prophet. She was one of the ladies who presented the petition to Governor Thomas Carlin at his residence in Quincy.

On June 29 1842, she married Joseph Smith as a plural wife for time and eternity, an event of "eternal import" to her: "The Prophet Joseph had taught me the principle of plural, or celestial marriage, and I was married to him for time and eternity. In consequence of the ignorance of most of the Saints, as well as the people of the world, on this subject, it was not mentioned only privately between the few whose minds were enlightened on the subject."[34]

After the martyrdom of the Prophet Joseph Smith, Eliza, prostrated with grief, sought the Lord with all the fervency of her soul to let her follow him to the grave, and was weighed down by her burden. As she lay awake, the Prophet appeared to her and told her that she must not continue to supplicate the Lord in that way, for it was not in accordance with the design of the Lord concerning her. The Prophet informed her that his life upon the earth was closed and that he had performed his mortal mission, but that her mission was not to come to an end for many years. He and the Lord desired her to live and assist in carrying on the great Latter-day work, which the Prophet had established. "She must be of good cheer, and help to cheer and lighten the burden of others. . . . She must turn her thoughts away from her own loneliness and seek to console her people in their bereavement and sorrow."[35]

How quickly and how well this brave woman heeded the admonition of her prophet-husband is shown by the fact that only four days following the tragic scene in Carthage she wrote a poem which pathetically and vividly described the assassination and exalted characters of the murdered brothers. The theme of her great poem is found in Revelation 6:9-11, which reads: "And when he had opened the fifth seal, I saw under the altar the souls of them that were slain for the word of God, and the testimony which they held."

The opening words of her noble poem are:

> Ye heavens attend! Let all the earth give ear!
> Let Gods and seraphs, men and angels hear
> The words on high—the universe shall know,
> What awful scenes are acted here below!
> Had nature's self a heart, her heart would bleed
> At the recital of so foul a deed;
> For never since the Son of God was slain
> Has blood so noble flowed from human vein
> As that which now on God for vengeance calls
> From "Freedom's" ground—from Carthage Prison
>   walls.[36]

A few months later, when President Brigham Young as president of the Council of Twelve took over the leadership of the Church, the poetess of Zion offered him encouragement in a cheering manner.

> A responsible station is surely thine
> And the weight of your calling can none define;
> Being called of the Lord, o'er the Twelve to preside,
> And with them o'er the Church and the world besides.
>
> * * *
>
> The Great Spirit of Truth will direct your ways;
> Generations to come will repeat your praise;
> When your work on earth is accomplished, you'll stand
> In your station appointed at God's right hand.[37]

Sister Eliza was one of the first of the Saints to leave Nauvoo in February 1846. This was her third exodus from a home for the gospel's sake. She traveled with the party of Stephen Markham, a staunch friend of her martyred husband. Certain unpleasant incidents and misfortunes befell the party which rendered it necessary for Eliza to drive a team of oxen from Mt. Pisgah to the Missouri River. True to her sympathetic and helpful nature she attended the sick, assisted in childbirth, and poured healing ointment into wounds, both mental and physical. It is from her pen that we learn of the suffering of the women—how, that first night out from Nauvoo, nine babies were born, and how she, along with other sisters, held pans over the bed of one dear soul to keep the rain off while a babe was brought into the world. And again, it was Sister Eliza who gave courage to the Saints with her songs of hope and cheer, which they would sing with zest and forget their inconveniences and discomfiture. One of these invigorating hymns exults:

> Although in woods and tents we dwell,
> Shout! shout! O camp of Israel;

No Christian mobs on earth can bind
Our thoughts, or steal our peace of mind.

Though we fly from vile aggression
We'll maintain our pure profession,
Seek a peaceable possession,
Far from Gentiles and oppression.

We'd better live in tents and smoke
Than wear the cursed Gentile yoke,
We'd better from our country fly
Than by mobbery to die—

The camp, the camp—its numbers swell—
Shout! shout! O camp of Israel!
The king, the Lord of hosts is near,
His armies guard our front and rear.[38]

Sister Eliza traveled to the Great Salt Lake Valley with the Jedediah M. Grant Company in 1847. Their company met President Young and many of the pioneers returning to Winter Quarters. From them she received a very favorable report of the new mountain Zion.

She spent the first winter in the valley. Food was scarce, and clothing was threadbare and patched. She worked feverishly with the other Saints during the summer of 1848, battling the crickets; and she with them, rejoiced and praised God when the seagulls came and devoured the loathsome insects.

After the final return of President Young to the valley in September 1848, he provided Eliza with a home. In 1849 she married him and remained a member of his household until her death. Exposures and hardships had racked her body, sapping her vitality and endurance, and she suffered from enfeebled health for many years.

When the Endowment House was dedicated in May 1855, President Young asked her to take charge of and preside over the sisters' work within this sacred building. Eliza reminded President Young of her poor health and expressed a doubt that she would be physically able to do the work required. The President assured her that her health would improve and that she would find joy in the labors to which the Lord had called her. This noble sister believed the man of God and accepted the call. Almost immediately her health improved, and she faithfully fulfilled this call as long as ordinance work was performed in the Endowment House. Her zealous involvement in the temple endowment won for her the title of "High Priestess."

In Nauvoo prior to her departure for the Salt Lake Valley, she had been recorder in the temple. In the Salt Lake Endowment House, she presided over the women's section, where she performed the holy ordinances for the faithful of the womanhood of the Church. She blessed them beyond the scope of the ceremonies themselves. As a matron in the Endowment House the sisters of Zion placed on Eliza an aura of sacredness and her officiating in the holy ordinances gave an atmosphere which surrounded her in the eyes of her contemporaries. Added to the gifts of the Spirit with which she was endowed, the temple calling was the official sanction and her title justified the reverence which was generally accorded her. Her message to the sisters always was, "We will do as we are directed by the priesthood."[39]

In 1866 the Relief Society was reorganized. At this time, each ward had its local organization and Sister Eliza was set apart as president over the entire sisterhood of the Church. For twenty-one years she held this position and retired only when failing health forced her to remain quietly at home a short time before her death in 1887.

In 1872-73 she had the privilege of traveling to the Holy Land with her brother Lorenzo, President George A. Smith, and others. While in Palestine, President Smith rededicated the land for the return of the Jews. Eliza was thrilled with all she saw. To walk over the same hills and vales, to stand on the same streets as Jesus had, and to gaze upon blue Galilee where the

Lord Jesus had experienced storm and calm was an
exciting experience for the poetess of Zion. Riding
horseback from the Fountain of Elisha, she left the
plains of Jericho and ascended into a wild, rocky moun-
tainous region to Jerusalem, and after a short stay in the
squalid village of Bethany where Mary and Martha
once entertained the Lord, her company approached
Jerusalem, passing the Garden of Gethsemane and
entering the "Holy City" through the Joffa Gate. Later
when she ascended the Mount of Olives on the east, rising several hundred feet above Jerusalem, she "spent a
happy hour surveying the 'Holy City.'" There she
penned her "Apostrophe to Jerusalem," the opening
lines being:

> Thou city with a cherished name,
> A name in garland drest,
> Adorned with ancient sacred fame
> As city of the blest.
> Thy rulers once, were mighty men,
> Thy sons, renowned in war;
> Thy smiles were sought and courted them
> By people from afar.
>
> * * *
>
> The Lord was with thee then, and deigned,
> In speech well understood,
> Through prophets, by His wisdom trained,
> To counsel for their good,
> Attracted by illustrious fame,
> As by a ruling star,
> To study wisdom, people came
> From other climes afar.[40]

Eliza felt satisfied with her visit to "that renowned
city of sacredly interesting histories of the past, and of
bright prophetic anticipation for the future, and in spite
of the deep sense of the curse of God resting on the land
and on the people, my feelings during our stay had
become so pleasantly associated with the scenic view of

the surroundings of this ancient site of time-honored memories that I realized a feeling of reluctance at bidding a final adieu."[41]

Her most memorable and precious view of the land where her Lord Jesus walked and taught was Galilee. While there she wrote on March 17, 1873:

> I have stood on the shore of the beautiful sea,
> The renowned and immortalized Galilee,
> When 'twas wrapp'd in repose, at eventide,
> Like a royal queen in her regal pride.
>
> * * *
>
> Again when the shades of night were gone,
> In the clear bright rays of the morning dawn,
> I walked on the bank of this self-same Sea
> Where once our Redeemer was wont to be.
> Where "Lord save, or I perish," was Peter's prayer,
> Befitting the weak, and the faithless elsewhere.
> And here while admiring this Scriptural Sea,
> Th' bold vista of Time brought th' past up to me."[42]

After returning home she saluted the ladies of Utah with thanks "for your faith and prayers." She reported to them that she, and her party of tourists, had traveled 12,000 miles by water and 13,000 miles by land without accident. Then she wrote, "What an honor to be associated with those who are co-workers with God in establishing a government of peace and purity." She had seen so much of the opposite on her travels.

Eliza's life was consecrated to gospel work and to the elevation of woman and her redemption from conditions she had long been held in, helping to lift her into that freedom of action and range of thought from which she had hitherto been excluded. As President of the Relief Society with her organizing faculty, she took the lead in the organizing of Young Ladies associations and Primary associations for children. Through these institutions the Lord has greatly blessed woman and she has become more heroic, for new light has dawned upon her mind, latent thoughts have been aroused, and higher aspirations awakened. This has given fuller expression and deeper meaning to her life work.

For the purpose of enlightening the nation regarding woman's position in the Mormon Church, six thousand women gathered in the tabernacle in Salt Lake City January 13, 1870. Eliza made a strong and brilliant speech. In it she said:

> Our enemies pretend that, in Utah, woman is held in a state of vassalage—that she does not act from choice, but by coercion—that we would even prefer to live elsewhere, were it possible for us to make our escape. What nonsense! We all know that if we wished we could leave at any time.
>
> I will now ask this assemblage of intelligent ladies. Do you know of any place on the earth, where woman has more liberty, and where she enjoys such high and glorious privileges as she does here as a Latter-day Saint? No! The very idea of a woman here in a state of slavery is a burlesque on good common sense. As women of God, filling high and responsible positions, performing sacred duties, women who stand not as dictators, but as counselors to their husbands, and who in the purest, noblest sense of refined womanhood, are truly their helpmates—we not only speak because we have a right, but justice and humanity demands we should.[43]

Before another month had elapsed, the Utah Legislature had passed a bill giving suffrage to women, and Eliza rejoiced in woman's political emancipation in Utah, which was next to the first commonwealth in the United States to give woman the political and social right belonging to her.

Through her years Eliza increased her role as leader and teacher of her sisters. She considered herself not only a poetess in Zion but a prophetess as well. On one occasion while visiting in the home of Rachel Ivins Grant with Emmeline B. Wells and Zina Young, she was given the gift of tongues and pronounced a blessing on Rachel's little son. Heber Jeddy Grant—that he would become a greater leader in the Church than his father Jedediah M. Grant, who was a counselor in the First Presidency. When she was well over 80 years of age, in a discourse in tongues, she said: "This is a great work and the Gospel is designed to draw all people together. We thought the days of our youth was the time of happiness and enjoyment. I can bear my testimony to my young sisters that the older I grow the happier I am."

Eliza R. Snow held no fear of death. Hers had been a life rich in experience and full in leadership fulfillment. She knew firmly that life would continue beyond the grave. Her last poetic composition revealed her anticipation of death: "Yes, immortality: that bosom word, to me has inspiration in it."

Sister Eliza died at the Lion House, 5 December 1887, when she was eighty-three years, ten months, and fourteen days old. She was buried in President Brigham Young's private cemetery on the hillside northeast of his family residence and the Eagle Gate.[44]

Her funeral services were held in the Assembly Hall on December 7. Ten speakers spoke in praise and honor of Sister Eliza. Her beautiful hymns were sung by the choir. In accordance with her wish, the stands were draped in white. Nothing black was seen. The opening number sung by the choir was her immortal hymn "O My Father."

A member of the First Presidency said:

> Morally, religiously and poetically, she seemed to be one of those perfect women that was prepared for the age, and to represent her sex in this great Latter-day work, and she nobly filled the mission for which she was appointed, and in which she took her place in the early days of this Church.45

The Poetess of Zion penned her own epitaph:

> 'Tis not the tribute of a sigh
> From tears that flow from pity's eye
> To weep for me when I am gone;
> No costly balm, no rich perfume—
> No vain sepulchral rite, I claim—
> No mournful knell—no marble tomb—
> No sculptur'd stone to tell my name.
> In friendship's memory let me live;
> I know no selfish wish beside,
> I ask no more. . . .
>
> * * *
>
> I feel the low responses roll
> Like far off echoes of the night,
> And whisper softly thro' my soul,
> I would not be forgotten quite.

Praises to Eliza flooded the newspapers and periodicals. The Deseret News ran columns extolling her contributions and virtues: "She has gone to mingle with the righteous who have kept the faith; to associate with her husband, the great prophet of the last dispensation. There was a marked harmony between the qualities of the heart and the gifts of the intellect of this remarkable woman. The purity of her life and nature necessarily rendered her a fit medium through whom the Holy Ghost could manifest those gifts and graces of the Gospel of the Redeemer."[46]

Eliza touched the hearts of thousands, yet her greatest influence is felt through her hymns touching sensitive souls. All minds and hearts are lifted heavenward by "O My Father," "How Great the Wisdom and the Love," "Behold the Great Redeemer Die," and "In Our Lovely Deseret." Church members still sing ten of her hymns as found in the current hymnal. Time may come and time may go, but Eliza Roxey Snow shall never be forgotten! She is timeless!

Notes

[1] A. A. Ramseyer, "Eliza Roxey Snow Smith," *The Utah Genealogical and Historical Magazine*, Vol. II, July 1911, p. 98.

[2] Orson F. Whitney, *History of Utah* (Salt Lake City: George Q. Cannon and Sons, 1892), Vol. IV, p. 573.

[3] Eliza R. Snow Smith, *Biography and Family Record of Lorenzo Snow* (Salt Lake City, Utah: Deseret News, 1884), p. 7.

[4] *The Life and Labors of Eliza R. Snow Smith* (Salt Lake City: Juvenile Instructor Office, 1888), p. 8.

[5] Andrew Jenson, *Biographical Encyclopedia*, (Salt Lake City: Arrow Press, 1920), Vol. 1, p. 695.

[6] Smith, p. 3.

[7] Smith, p. 4.

[8] Whitney, *History*, p. 574.

[9] *Life and Labors, op cit*, p. 7.

[10] Whitney, *History*, p. 573.

[11] *Ibid.*

[12] Ellen Wallace, "Eliza Roxey Snow Smith," *Young Woman's Journal* 21:8-13, 1910.

[13] Whitney

[14] *The Western Galaxy*, March 1888, p. 142.

[15] Edward W. Tullidge, *The Women of Mormondom*, (New York: Tullidge-Crandall, 1877), p. 64.

[16] Nicholas G. Morgan, *Eliza R. Snow, An Immortal: Selected Writings of Eliza R. Snow* (Salt Lake City, Utah: Nicholas G. Morgan Sr. Foundation, 1957), p. 6.

[17] *Ibid.*

[18] Eliza R. Snow, *Poems, Religious, Historical, and Political* (Liverpool, England, 1856 and Salt Lake City, Utah, 1877), 2 vols. Vol. 1, pp. 3, 4, 6.

[19] Eliza R. Snow Smith, *Biography*, p. 5.

[20] *Ibid.*, p. 5.

[21] *Ibid.*

[22] Jenson, p. 694.

[23] Snow, *Poems*, p. 15.

[24] Thomas C. Romney, *The Life of Lorenzo Snow* (Salt Lake City Utah: Sugarhouse Press, 1955), p. 9.

[25] Smith, p. 6.

26 Romney, p. 13.

27 Smith, p. 6.

28 Romney, p. 2.

29 Smith, p. 25.

30 Snow, *Poems*, pp. 7-8.

31 Whitney, *History* p. 574. See also Smith, p. 11.

32 Snow, *Poems*, p. 60.

33 Keith and Ann Terry, *Eliza* (Santa Barbara, California: Butterfly Publishing Co., 1981), pp. 35-36.

34 Eliza R. Snow, Diary and Notebook (sometimes called Nauvoo Journal). L.D.S. Church Archives, Salt Lake City, Utah. June 29, 1842.

35 Jenson, p. 695.

36 Smith, p. 80.

37 Snow, *Poems*, pp. 155-56.

38 Snow, *Poems*, pp. 161-62.

39 23 April 1883. Eliza R. Snow's Papers. L.D.S. Church Archives.

40 Correspondence with Palestine Tourists: A Series of Letters by George A. Smith, Lorenzo Snow, Paul A. Schettler and Eliza R. Snow. Deseret News Printing, Salt Lake City, 1875, pp. 241-242.

41 *Ibid.*, p. 261.

42 *Ibid.*, pp. 285-286.

43 A. H. Ramseyer, p. 101.

44 Jenson, p. 697.

45 *Life and Labors* p. 21.

46 *The Latter-day Saint's Millennial Star*, Vol. 50, No. 1, 2 January 1888.

"Little Children, How She Loved Them"

Aurelia Spencer Rogers:
Mother of the Primary

Abraham Lincoln once observed that God must love the common people because he made so many of them. Generally, it is the person with unusual talents, ability, wealth, or exceptional heroism who wins acclaim and makes his or her niche in the annals of history. But in the chronicles of the Church of Jesus Christ in these Latter-days there are hidden away many untold stories of common people who lived simply, yet extraordinarily; who were not called especially to any important position but who humbly and almost unobservedly made a lasting contribution to the building of the Kingdom of God. Among those who have performed such service was Aurelia Spencer Rogers.

Her biographer wrote, "Her life was as simple and humble as a sparrow's."[1] She was left motherless at twelve; then she and her older sister Ellen cared for four younger children.

As a child she fell from the hay loft, injuring her stomach, and from that time on she suffered with a chronic stomach disorder. In her childhood she had the habit of walking in her sleep, until one night after her arrival in Salt Lake Valley she knocked over a small cabinet. The clatter awakened her, so shocking and frightening her that it cured her of sleepwalking.

With her brothers and sisters, she crossed the plains under the care of Brigham Young in the summer of 1848, as their father was in England on a mission. In the pioneer company was a boy not much older than Aurelia, a laddie from bonnie Scotland named Thomas Rogers, who was driving a yoke of oxen. She became acquainted with Tom—often walking by his side as he "geed and hawed" the plodding oxen.

Three years later, when Aurelia was seventeen, this acquaintance of the plains which had ripened into romance culminated in marriage. Aurelia bore Tom twelve children. Five died in infancy—three in succession. One can imagine the anguish and sorrow which filled Aurelia's soul over this tremendous loss. After the death of her fifth child she said:

> I almost lost faith in God; for once in my life, I even doubted the existence of a Supreme Being.
>
> One day while reflecting on these things, one of my father's letters came to my mind, wherein he said, "Trust in God though he slay you!" I caught at the suggestion, which had surely been given by the Spirit of the Lord, and went to Him in prayer, asking Him to forgive me for my lack of faith, and to grant me strength to endure, feeling that I would put my trust in Him henceforth and forever.[2]

Meditating upon this harrowing experience and her rededication to her Maker, she concluded that the people of God must pass through much tribulation to prove whether they will trust in Him to the end. She was led to understand that the sufferings of the Saints of God might be likened to that of those clinging to the iron rod in the dream of Father Lehi as recorded in I Nephi 8. The way before them could not be seen, but by holding fast to the Word of God "they finally reach the tree of life, partake of the fruit and are happy."[3]

After following the counsel of her father and putting her trust in the God of her father, she was blessed with children that lived, and she enjoyed blessings beyond her expectations.

Aurelia Spencer Rogers did not do any of the things usually considered to constitute greatness; and yet her name will live as long as there are children in the Church of Christ. She is the original mother of the Primary Association. She loved children; she was concerned about all children. She dedicated her little book *Life Sketches* to children—to her children and all the children of the Latter-day Saints.

> Our children are our jewels;
> We have counted well the cost;
> May their angels ever guard them,
> And not one child be lost.[4]

That was the lifelong prayer of Sister Rogers.

When she passed beyond the veil in her eighty-seventh year, she left behind a model life as a pattern for every Primary girl. Her life taught them to be neat, for she was a meticulous housekeeper; her actions taught them neighborliness, for her fellow townspeople adored her. When children sing "I Have Two Little Hands," they could well remember the busy hands of their original Primary mother who was an expert seamstress and who always looked to see if she could help someone in need. Children today who tend to be selfish, thinking only of themselves and what luxuries they might enjoy, can find greater happiness if they model their lives after that of Sister Rogers, who walked through life "with queenly simplicity ever thinking of others."

Even when death beckoned her, she begged her family and friends to place no profusion of flowers on her bier. "I would like just a few simple blossoms from my own garden," she requested. "If anyone has money to spend for flowers for me, it would make me happier to have it given to comfort someone in need."[5]

Well did a relative write in poetic vein of this remarkable, unselfish Saint:

> In lives, however humble, there yet gleams
> Some truth or lesson—some bright light that streams
> Through all the troubled seeming, and dim ways
> To 'lumine earth's dark problems with its rays.
> The greatest heroes are not always those
> Whose names are blazoned, or whose life-page glows
> With tales of martial glory, public pride
> And titled honor—in earth's spaces wide,
> And through all ages there have dwelt unsung
> A multitude of souls whose life chords strung
> To noblest music—uncrowned Lords of earth—
> Brave men and women—Kings and queens of worth.
>
> —Josephine Spencer

Aurelia was born of noble parents from sturdy New England stock. Her father, Orson Spencer, was born in Massachusetts; her mother, Catherine Curtis Spencer, was born in New York. At fourteen her father contracted typhus fever—the same disease which young Joseph Smith endured—which nearly cost him his life. By another coincidence, like Joseph Smith, Orson's fever settled in his leg, causing lameness for life.

Being lame left Orson unfit for active, strenuous pursuits in life so he became educated for the ministry. He proved himself an apt scholar and was one of the few men of his time to acquire two college degrees.

In the year that the Church was organized, in fact, in the very month of its organization, Orson married pretty Catherine Curtis, nine years his junior, who had a beautiful singing voice. As a Baptist minister, Orson Spencer received a salary large enough to "keep his family comfortably."

Aurelia was born in Deep River, Connecticut, on 4 October 1834. She was the third child and the third daughter. The eldest daughter had died at two. Aurelia's earliest recollections were of living in Middlefield, Massachusetts, in a large two-story house facing east. She remembered the snow drifting so high that she could step from the upper window out onto the frozen snow bank.

She had been told that God lived in the heavens above. So she stepped out of doors one day and looked up into the atmosphere expecting to see her Heavenly Father walking among the clouds. When she failed to see him she was very disappointed.

Aurelia was very fond of her name. She had been named for Aurelia Read, a friend of her parents, who gave young Aurelia a little red-covered New Testament for a keepsake. It was one of Aurelia's prized possessions.[6]

With glowing pride she remembered Ellen, her sister immediately older than she, at the age of seven years "spelling down" the whole school of much older boys and girls.

When Aurelia herself was seven, Uncle Daniel Spencer visited from West Stockbridge, about a day's journey away, with the purpose of preaching Mormonism to his minister brother and his wife. He and Aurelia's parents sat up late every night for days, conversing upon the principles of the newly restored gospel. One evening Catherine said to her husband, "Orson, you know this is true."[7] He acknowledged that she was right and they both shed tears, feeling the influence of the Holy Spirit in their midst. Shortly afterward they were both baptized. Almost all of the Spencer family joined the Church; but as Aurelia states in her *Life Sketches,* "Not one of my mother's relatives ever joined the Church, and they felt quite bitter toward my father for taking their beloved one away, fearing they might never see her again; and so it was proved, altho' father visited them afterward."[8]

Orson Spencer journeyed to Nauvoo, followed soon afterward by the family. One of Aurelia's Nauvoo memories is of Joseph Smith visiting their home and exclaiming, when her saw her baby sister, Lucy, "Oh, what a little black head!" Then he laid his hand upon the little black-haired baby and blessed her.[9] She also remembered caring for James Hendricks, who had been shot and crippled by the Missouri mobs, so incapacitated that he was unable to dress himself. "For more than thirty years Brother Hendricks lived on in that condition—a living martyr for the sake of his religion." Another neighbor was Amanda Smith, a heroine of the Haun's Mill Massacre. Observing the faith of these who had suffered so intensely and the love they had one for another and for the gospel caused Aurelia to cherish her newly espoused religion more dearly.

Aurelia would have been a very capable teacher with the right training and opportunities. As a child, she would arrange sticks in rows, pretending they were students, and then instruct them in some important phase of learning. On one occasion when she was drilling her pupils in her Uncle Hyrum's woodshed, she happened to look through an opening in the boards at the back of the shed: "O, horror! I saw my cousin Charles standing close by the corner, listening to my oratory and ready to burst with laughter. He did not know that he had been seen, but school was dismissed rather suddenly, and I ran for the house."[10]

In Nauvoo, Aurelia also met two girls who became lifelong friends: Mary Ann Stearns, a stepdaughter of Parley P. Pratt, and Ellen Pratt, whose father, Addison Pratt, was on a five-year mission to the South Sea Islands.

Aurelia's father was very active in civic as well as in religious affairs in Nauvoo. He was selected alderman in the city government, taught school, and operated a small store. He was sent on a short mission to the eastern states. When he returned, Grandfather and Grandmother Spencer came with him. They lived with Aurelia's father and died within a year of one another.

Aurelia's grandmother smoked a pipe and often asked Aurelia to light it for her. In doing this little service for her grandmother, Aurelia learned to smoke and liked it very much. Whenever she saw anyone smoking, she craved a few whiffs herself. She tells us that she innocently indulged in this habit at intervals for several years before she suddenly realized that such a habit was detrimental. She says, "There was a monitor within that told me it was wrong, and what it would lead to if persisted in: I should be, if I lived, an old lady smoker. This thought disgusted me, for I never did like to see women smoke."[11] It was a struggle for her to drop the habit, but she triumphed over it.

In later years when she was a teacher in the Primary Association, she did everything in her power to discourage her Primary children from the use of tobacco, with its attendant evils. Her own experience with the habit and her will power to overcome taught her important lessons.

One evening during her stay in Nauvoo, she and her closest girl friends were going to Mary Ann's house when they saw Brother Parley, in company with two ladies, going to a concert. Mary Ann suggested following her stepfather and trying to get into the concert, so Aurelia and Ellen were game and went along. They came to the door of the music hall in single file. Mary Ann followed Brother Pratt and when the doorman stopped her, she said, "I am Parley Pratt's daughter," and passed in. Ellen said, "I am her [Mary Ann's] cousin." Aurelia's did not know what to say but finally blurted out, "I am some relation; I don't know what." The doorman smiled and permitted her to enter.[12]

A sad memory was having her father lift her up to the window of the Mansion House, through which she saw the lifeless forms of Joseph and Hyrum Smith. She helped carry water when the temple caught on fire, and she wept when her baby sister, Chloe, died with whooping cough.

All of this was prelude to the exodus which began in the cold winter month of February, 1846.

The greatest sorrow came to young Aurelia soon afterward—the passing of her angel mother who was only thirty-five, "a victim to the cares and hardships of persecution." Aurelia's father, writing in third person in an account for his children, painted a pathetic picture of the last illness and passing of his beloved companion:

> Under the influence of a severe cold, she gradually wasted away, telling her children, from time to time, how she wanted them to live and conduct themselves, when they should become motherless and pilgrims in a strange land. To her companion she would some- times say, "I think you will have to give me up and let me go." As her little ones would often inquire at the door of the wagon, "How is Mama? Is she any better?" she would turn to her husband, who sat by the side endeavoring to keep the severities of rain and cold from her with, "Oh, you dear little children, how I do hope you will fall into kind hands when I am gone." A night or two before she died, she said to her husband, with unwonted animation, "A heavenly messenger has appeared to me tonight, and told me that I had done and suffered enough, and that he had now come to convey me to a mansion of gold."
>
> Soon after, she said she wished her husband to call the children and other friends to her bedside, that she might give them a parting kiss; which being done, she said to her companion, "I love you more than ever, but you must let me go. I only want to live for your sake, and that of our children." When asked if she had any- thing to say to her father's family, she replied emphatically, "Charge them to obey the gospel."[13]

Aurelia's mother had infused the purest and loftiest virtues into the minds of her children and not only exemplified the beautiful order of heaven, but made her domestic circle when it was at its best, the most sublime paradise on earth. A member of the High Council who often observed her in the Temple of the Lord in Nauvoo, where she loved to linger and feast on the joys of that holy place, said, "I never saw a countenance more inexpressibly serene and heavenly than hers."[14] His love and affection for his companion led Orson Spencer to the following poetic expression:

> Oh she was young who won my yielding heart;
> No power of genius, nor the pen's art
> Could half the beauties of her mind portray
> Even when inspired: and how can this my lay?
> Two eyes that spoke what language ne'er could do.
> Soft as twin violets, moist with early dew.
>
> In sylph-like symmetry her form combined
> To prove the fond endearment of her mind,
> While on her brow, benevolence and love
> Sat meekly, like two emblems from above;
> And every thought that had creation there,
> But made her face still more divinely fair.

Orson Spencer wrote his sketch so that "his children, now in the wilderness for the testimony of Jesus," would have a permanent reminder of their mother, "lest time should obliterate from their young and tender minds the recollections of their mother's person, and some of her virtues."[15]

Following the sad return to Nauvoo, Aurelia's mother was buried beside her infant daughter. The father took his six little children to Winter Quarters on the west bank of the Missouri. Here he labored feverishly to build a cabin and to gather fuel and food for them before he left on a mission to the British Isles. They were ill when he embraced them, leaving them to the care of the Lord and a good couple, James and Mary Bullock.

The door of the Bullock cabin faced the Spencers' door and was only a few feet away, but the children kept house by themselves, fourteen-year-old "Ellen acting the part of a little mother."[16] Another neighbor, Jane Dudson, helped the girls cut out dresses and sew them. Aurelia, from careful observation, became very proficient in the art of dressmaking at a young age.

The Spencer children got through the first winter pretty well, since their father had provided for their needs by leaving them eight cows as well as a horse, which was sold for provisions. Caroline Pratt taught a school which the Spencer children attended quite regularly. Aurelia even remembers happy evenings playing "mumblety peg" on the dirt floor, impromptu spelling bees, and story-telling sessions. Orson Spencer sent money and letters filled with counsel and encouragement to his struggling children via travelers. They never received any of the money because the travelers pocketed it, but they profited by the counsel and their father's loving encouragement such as:

> Now, my beloved children, love one another, and strive to please each other, and don't mind little offenses, but forgive and bear with each other's faults. Pray often and be not angry nor contentious with anybody. . . . When you are not well, fast and eat light food. Wash your bodies often in pure water and comb your heads—that from the head to the feet you may be clean and healthy. Go to school as much as you can— Trust to the counsel of those who are set over you in the Lord. . . . Never yield to sin or do anything that you would be ashamed to ask God about or tell me of. Let no one entice you to do wrong, whoever it may be. . . . Learn to trust in the Lord for all good things, and to be thankful for all favors.[17]

The Bullocks lost two children to illness that year, but every child in the Spencer family was spared.

As spring came on and their provisions became more scanty, the Spencers had nothing but corn meal to eat. Many a night Aurelia would retire without supper, hoping by morning she would be hungry enough to eat what she called "our poor fare." Wilford Woodruff, learning of their destitute circumstances, visited them and supplied their wants.[18]

Orson, ever concerned about his family, wrote President Young and requested him to take special care of his children. "Don't forget to give a good piece of love to the six orphan children somewhat south of you on Main street. I sometimes think of the lambs on a stormy day because some of them had not very warm fleeces for cold weather."

In the spring of 1848, Brigham Young took the little family west to the Rocky Mountains. Before their departure their father warned them "to be cautious in regard to hostile Indians, serpents and dangerous roots and herbs. Do not walk out at night away from the camp. You will scarcely be saved with the utmost faith, diligence and economy. My anxieties about you from the time you leave till I see you will be unceasingly great." In addition, he placed this charge on Ellen and Aurelia: "Seemingly beyond your years, be womanly, kind and patient, act the part of mother to the younger children. Teach them good principles and instruct them how to act. . . . Never forget or slight my counsel, for . . . I write to you according to the mind of God."[19]

Only once while crossing the plains did Aurelia disregard her father's counsel. While her company was camped on Looking-Glass Creek, a small tributary to the Platte River, Aurelia and about a dozen of her companions decided to walk down to the Platte one bright moonlight night to bathe. An older woman, Mima Young, accompanied them, standing guard on the bank while the girls bathed.

As they splashed about, enjoying themselves, one of the girls, innocently enough, suggested that they play "baptize." Some of the others consented and were ducked under the water. This game was interrupted, however, by one of them exclaiming, "See! what is that coming?" The startled girls saw something white and strange coming slowly across the river toward them. Frightened, they dashed out of the water screaming and saw the object float up stream and disappear up Looking-Glass Creek which emptied into the Platte River.[20]

Naturally, the girls made many excited conjectures about the frightening object, but all agreed that it was certainly a warning against their game. They had also disobeyed counsel by going so far away from camp at night. This experience caused Aurelia much sober reflection. But the mystery of what the girls had seen was never solved.

Arriving in Salt Lake Valley after five weary months on the plains, the Spencer children were greeted and cared for by Uncle Daniel. He had built them a single floorless room in the fort which consisted of log rooms joined together until a square was formed, with gateways to enter through. The stove was tucked into one corner and on this they baked their biscuits. When the biscuits were done, the family would sit around the stove and eat them.

That first winter in the Valley, Aurelia industriously sewed dresses for the family and neighbors. She also braided some very attractive bracelets and necklaces out of horsehair which made a little welcome money for the family. She and Ellen attended writing school two evenings a week taught by Hiram B. Clawson. They also attended meetings and dancing parties.

In the summer of 1849, word came that Orson Spencer, their father, was on his way home:

The day arrived, and the six Spencer children, the oldest now seventeen and the youngest seven, counted the hours. It was late in September. Dusk came, then darkness—but no father. Disappointed, they blew out the candles and tumbled into their beds. They did not sleep, however. The letdown was too stinging for that.

Then, of a sudden almost, they heard wagon wheels

rumbling at their gate and the sound of a man's voice commanding the horses to stop. The children listened intently and heard a knock on the door. A man's voice inquired the direction to Dr. Richards's home. Aurelia was thrown off guard, she says, and commenced giving the requested direction, but Ellen called out, "Pa, is that you?" What joy and excitement prevailed in that little room as they hurriedly opened the door, lighted a candle and embraced their dear father who had been absent from them so long.[21]

On 27 March 1851, Aurelia married Thomas Rogers, her sweetheart of the plains, and moved north to Farmington. Farmington was a scattering of a few log huts. The groom and his teenage bride moved into a two-room log cabin with a roof of willows and dirt. One room had the convenience of two small windows. On the floor was a homemade rug, the gift of the bridegroom's mother. Aurelia's dressing table was a dry goods box fitted onto two pegs driven into the log wall. She draped it with a white sheet and put her freshly ironed clothes inside. On top of her makeshift dressing table she placed her books. She was an experienced cook, but she did her housekeeping without a stove, cooking over the fireplace. Her furniture consisted of four chairs, a table and a cupboard. She carried water from a stream at the base of a hill. When her broom wore out, she gathered willows and tied them together. For cleaning the woodwork she used sand and a rag.

Aurelia writes of this time: "A new life was opening up before me. I was just merging from girlhood into womanhood, being in my seventeenth year. I little realized the care and the responsibility of looking after a home of my own. Like many other new beginners, there was nothing for me but the bright side to look upon, and I imagined myself equal to the emergency."[22]

On Sundays, Aurelia and Thomas and, very soon, their children, attended church in a wardhouse sixteen by eighteen feet, situated near the creek, its roof of willows and dirt, its floor of split logs. A large fireplace kept the ward members warm in winter. Mud chinking between the logs protected them against the canyon winds. One strong wind in Farmington blew President Brigham Young's buggy over during his visit there. The Prophet rebuked the gale and the winds were calmer thereafter.

Four years after settling in Farmington there was a grasshopper plague. Green fields turned yellow and barren. Wheat was scarce. Thomas sold a horse for twenty dollars. With the money he purchased flour. The little family subsisted on a bran bread diet.

Indian threats increased, and in 1854, the people of Farmington put up a protecting wall, six feet and a half high and four feet thick around the townsite.

At a General Conference, Aurelia's Thomas was called on a mission to Great Britain. Her two older sons, seventeen and fifteen, cared for their mother and the younger children while their father was in England. The fifteen-year-old son was named Lorce. In later years he moved to Snowflake, Arizona where he became a living legend.

Aurelia reared seven children, in addition to the five others she lost in infancy. She had not the conveniences we enjoy today, but with all her hardships, trials, privations, disappointments, and bereavements, she could say, "With the exception of certain times of trial, I was happy as a bird."[23] One of the keys to this happiness was given her by her saintly father (who died suddenly in St. Louis while serving a mission) when once he wrote:

> I daily and hourly hope to please my Heavenly Father better than I have in times past. Can I but become pure in heart, I have the immutable promise that I shall see God and come back into His presence and be acknowledged among His worthy sons. . . . I know that my Heavenly Father wants me to exercise unwavering faith in Him with all my heart. . . . I have realized that I never can be truly happy only in doing His will, even

though it be unto death. Herein is true happiness, riches, honor and eternal glory of the Saints.[24]

And Aurelia followed this prescribed course of happiness. She lived to please her Heavenly Father; she exercised faith in him; she strove to do his will.

When she was in her early forties, with her own family mostly raised, she observed the rowdiness and mischief of the Farmington boys and thought seriously about the problem. These little fellows were allowed to stay out late at nights; and they played pranks on older people, often doing damage to property. This mischief may have seemed innocent enough to many in Farmington, but Aurelia pondered, "What can be done to look after the spiritual welfare of the children?" The bishop, concerned about the same problem, called a mothers' meeting and discussed the necessity of training the children. Little results came from this meeting but "a fire seemed to burn within"[25] Aurelia. She conceived the idea of starting an organization for little boys in which they could learn how to behave.

In March of 1878 when Eliza R. Snow visited the Farmington Relief Society, Aurelia expressed her concern over the rough, careless ways of the boys to Eliza. "What will our girls do for good husbands, if this state of things continues?" she asked. "Could there not be an organization for little boys, and have them trained to make better men?"

Sister Snow promised to take this important matter up with the Quorum of the Twelve. She did; and shortly afterward, Bishop John Hess received a letter giving the approval of President John Taylor and the Twelve for a children's organization to begin in Farmington. The bishop asked Aurelia to preside over this organization. With characteristic humility, Aurelia responded that she "felt willing, but very incompetent." On Sunday, 11 August 1878, Aurelia S. Rogers was set apart to preside over a Primary Association in Farmington, named at Eliza R. Snow's suggestion and designed to include girls as well as boys."[26]

The children were taught obedience, faith in God, prayer, punctuality, and good manners. "We always endeavored to impress the children," says Aurelia, "with the fact that home is the place to begin to practice all good things."[27] Many of the boys and girls put into practice what they were taught in Primary. Sister Aurelia was pleased especially when "we heard from several of the mothers afterwards, who had noticed quite a change for the better in their children."

Aurelia Rogers saw her Primary organization spread throughout the territory. Her Primary children loved her because she loved them. They showered her with a quilt, a plush-covered album, and a framed testimonial. They loved to catch her by surprise. One of these surprise parties became a veritable town celebration with the Silver Band on parade, festivities, speeches, and a program featuring a song written especially for the occasion.

When Aurelia's husband, Thomas, died suddenly of a stroke and Aurelia was prostrated with sorrow and strain, the Primary children at conference in Richfield offered a special prayer in her behalf. Sister Rogers said, "And I thank the children everywhere who remembered me in that way." She expressed her thoughts of and her love for her Primary children in poetry:

> Little children how I love them,
> Pure, bright spirits from above;
> What would heaven be without them?
> Or this world, without their love?
>
> Yet these little angel spirits,
> Sometimes have been heard to say
> Naughty words, use impure language.
> While in anger at their play.

> Little thinking of the Tempter,
> Ever standing near,
> Waiting, watching to mislead them,
> From the ways of truth, I fear.
>
> Then dear children, be ye always
> Pure and holy day by day;
> Ask the Lord to guard and keep you
> In the straight and narrow way.
>
> Never grieve your Heavenly Watchers
> By a coarse or impure word;
> Nor forget to pray for loved ones,
> For the children's prayers are heard.[28]

The greatest tribute came to Sister Rogers when she was made a delegate to the Woman's Suffrage Convention in Atlanta, Georgia, with all expenses paid. In the comfort of a train, she traveled much of the same rough country that she had walked over as a girl alongside an ox team. "Life in Atlanta's plush Aragon Hotel was breathtaking to the delegate from Farmington. Here were electric lights, elevators, colored bellhops and waiters who, at the press of a button, brought tumblers of ice water."[29] She was honored at the convention with an appointment to the Resolutions Committee.

Aurelia S. Rogers had endured more than her share of trials and sorrows, but all these cruel twists of life had not embittered her. Rather, they mellowed her with a sweetness that was "enduring like the costlier perfumes." She developed a faith "that was constant and quiet and warming as the sun."[30] She once described her philosophy in these words: "If God seems to withhold his blessings, and your prayers are not answered in a way you desire, can you feel to acknowledge his hand even in this, and say, 'Thy will be done and not mine'? This is what I call trusting in God."[31]

The lover and developer of youth passed quietly to her well-earned reward on 19 August 1922. She was beloved of her neighbors and highly respected by the authorities of the Church, both those locally and those of the general leaders. She was three years short of ninety, and her passing came six days after the forty-fourth anniversary of the organization she had begun in order to save boys and girls.

No greater tribute could be paid to Aurelia than is found in the sentiments of love expressed in a song called "Greetings to Sister Aurelia S. Rogers":

> A ship over life's ocean was sailing
> Which brought to us tidings of joy;
> A message from heaven to greet us,
> Glad tidings to each girl and boy.
> It was brought to her whom we honor,
> In whose presence we mingle today,
> With hearts filled with love and devotion,
> To cheer her on life's checkered way.
> We honor thy dear name, thy words we revere,
> Our memories gratefully twine
> Round the children's bright anchor established by thee,
> Which will now and eternally shine.
>
> The Primary armies are marshalled in line,
> While they bless thee, Jehovah they praise;
> The sweet songsters join in their anthems of joy
> For the mercies of these latter days.
> They are marching with step firm and fearless,
> Bravely seeking the Lord in their youth,
> The victory is theirs if they faithfully remain
> And continue to struggle for truth.
>
> The gold of the earth would be worthless
> Compared to the truths you have taught,
> A statue we rear while you're living,
> More sure than in marble well wrought,
> If we heed the sweet counsel you've given
> And practice it ever with care,
> We will meet with our blessed Redeemer
> And with love's tokens honor you there.[32]

Notes

[1] Wendell J. Ashton, *Theirs is the Kingdom* (Salt Lake City: Bookcraft, 1945), p. 5.

[2] Aurelia S. Rogers, *Life Sketches* (Salt Lake City: Geo. Q. Cannon & Sons Co., 1898), p. 180.

[3] Rogers, p. 180.

[4] Rogers, p. iii.

[5] Ashton, p. 7.

[6] Rogers, "Childhood Days," p. 12.

[7] Rogers, p. 16.

[8] *Ibid.*, p. 21.

[9] Ashton, p. 14.

[10] Rogers, p. 19.

[11] Rogers, pp. 27-28.

[12] Rogers, pp. 29-30.

[13] Preston Nibley, *Exodus to Greatness* (Salt Lake City: Deseret News Press, 1947), pp. 133-134; "Memoirs of John R. Young, Utah Pioneer, 1847," written by himself, Salt Lake City, *The Deseret News*, 1920, pp. 17-18.

[14] *Ibid.*

[15] Rogers, p. 40. See also Andrew Jenson, *Biographical Encyclopedia*, 3 vols. (Salt Lake City: Arrow Press, 1920), Vol. 1, p. 338.

[16] Rogers, Ch. vi. Sister Ellen, the "Little Mother," p. 47.

[17] Rogers, pp. 61-71.

[18] Ashton, p. 20.

[19] Rogers, p. 71.

[20] *Ibid.*, p. 78.

[21] Ashton, p. 29.

[22] Rogers, p. 124.

[23] Rogers, p. 126.

[24] Rogers, p. 134.

[25] Preston Nibley, *Stalwarts of Mormonism* (Salt Lake City: Deseret Book Co., 1954), p. 171.

[26] Rogers, p. 212.

[27] Rogers, p. 216.

[28] Rogers, pp. 282-283.

[29] Ashton, p. 42.

[30] Ashton, p. 43.

[31] *Ibid.*

[32] Lucy A. Clark, "Greeting to Sister Aurelia S. Rogers," *Juvenile Instructor*, September 1889, Vol. 24.

Elizabeth Claridge McCune
A Heroic Woman of True Greatness

Here is a woman who was born in England, who grew up in the rustic town of Nephi, Utah, who lived in five states and in two countries, traveled in many parts of the world, sharing with many people the gospel of Jesus Christ. She was one of the first telegraph operators in Utah Territory. She went through all the trials and privations of settling the barren wastes of western America. She married a man who was born in India and was the mother of nine children. Her husband became a multi-millionaire, and together they built a mansion, which became known worldwide, on the brow of a hill on north Main Street in Salt Lake City .

Elizabeth served on two Church general boards for women, and was very popular in local theatricals. She was appointed by the Governor to be a trustee of the Agricultural College of Logan, and acted as vice president of the board, the first woman in the United States to occupy that high public trust. She acquired many friends and grappled them to her heart with hooks of steel. She offered a warm and generous hospitality to any numbered among her numerous friends. To a band of hostile Indians on a lonely ranch, she dispensed hospitality in the shape of bread and molasses; in one of London's most exclusive hotels she hosted Mormon missionaries just out of their teens, and was in turn entertained by members of the House of Parliament.

Elizabeth gave to the young women of the Church their colors of gold and green. She loved beauty and was a real artist. Her sense of humor and ability to see the funny side were a source of inspiration and joy to her associates. She contributed so much to the well-being of humanity, and labored so untiringly as a genealogist and ordinance worker in the Salt Lake Temple, that a living prophet applauded her with being "one of the great women of the Church in the latter days."

Reminiscences in the life of Elizabeth Claridge McCune

To the fifteen-year-old Elizabeth Claridge no place on earth seemed so precious as dear old Nephi—the village bearing the name of an ancient American prophet.

Shortly after the Civil War broke out, the Overland Telegraph Line was completed to Salt Lake City. President Brigham Young sent the first message over the lines east to J. H. Wade, president of the company, congratulating him "upon the completion of the over-land telegraph line west to this city." He then declared, "Utah has not seceded, but is firm for the Constitution and laws of our happy country."

President Wade replied that he was gratified that the first message to pass over the line "should express so unmistakably the patriotism and Union-loving senti-ments of yourself and people."[8]

Telegraph lines were erected to many of the settle-ments in Utah Territory, Nephi being one of them. In the summer of 1866 Elizabeth and her friends, Elizabeth Parks, Hetty Page and Mary Neff were called by the bishop of Nephi to study telegraphy. Their teacher was William Bryan, sent there by President Brigham Young to teach these teenage girls how to operate the switches. Elizabeth, called Lizzette by her friends, was assigned to Mona, a town twelve miles north of Nephi to operate the switchboard. She enjoyed being a telegraph operator. As she had a lot of time to herself, she decided to write her life history up to her teenage period.

Elizabeth noted as she began her history that she was born February 19, 1852 at Hemel, Hempstead, Hertz, England. Her father's people were comfortable as far as this world's goods were concerned. Better still, she was well born, descending from noble ancestors, for whom in later life she gathered genealogy and labored as proxy in temple ordinances in their behalf. She had few opportunities for education; but "she had a most precious inheritance—the spiritual gift of ladyship; and that means gentle behavior, a kind spirit and consideration for others."[9]

Her parents, Samuel Claridge and Charlotte Joy, joined the Church of Jesus Christ of Latter-day Saints in 1851, and Elizabeth was eleven months old when they emigrated to America. They sacrificed their present comfortable conditions and prospects of considerable wealth in the old world, and willingly grasped the toils and privations incident to the settlement and building of a new country. This they willingly did out of loyalty to their convictions. They arrived in Utah in the fall of 1853 and settled in Nephi.

Elizabeth's girlhood was spent in Nephi. She was industrious, diligent, and a happy worker in the pioneer arts and crafts. These attracted many friends. Among her much loved friends were Mary Ellen Love, Bessie Jeffries, Belle Parks, and Hetty Grace. Mary Ellen Love remembered those happy days in Nephi and said of Elizabeth, "She could spin six skeins of yard in a summer's day." She and her friends sometimes had their spinning wheels in the same room and worked together for company. They were never idle—sewing, knitting, crocheting or doing chores. Lizzette milked the family cows and was a hard worker. And there was also the fun side of her life, playing, walking, riding horses, and in the wintertime sleighing and dancing.

She was well known as the gifted and favorite actress of the Home Dramatic Troupe. She would tell with delight of playing opposite President Anton H. Lund when he was a boy. Lizzette was quick at repartee, humorous and full of droll sayings. She had the adroit talent to mimic anyone so perfectly that her friends could identify the boy, girl or adult she was imitating by her dramatic portrayal of them. One of her close friends remembered, "We youngsters nearly killed ourselves laughing at her impersonations." Elizabeth was very kindhearted and considerate and did not impersonate to hurt anyone, but simply to make fun for the crowd. In all their work, play and worship, Elizabeth was the leader and she brought happiness to all her friends with her unselfish, mirthful and gentle personality.

Then in the fall of 1856 the Major Matthew McCune family (consisting of the mother Sarah, and the three sons, Henry, Alfred and Edward) came to Nephi from Calcutta, India. Alfred was born in Calcutta in East India, April 8, 1849. His father was serving in the British army in Calcutta where he learned of the restored gospel from two sailor boys, each eighteen years of age. Major McCune and his wife entertained sailors from the British Navy in the huge mansion of forty rooms which they called the bungalow. He and Captain Meik wrote Elder Lorenzo Snow, president over the Italian Mission, requesting literature on the restored gospel. After the literature arrived and was carefully read, three men and two women were converted to the gospel. In 1851, another sailor arrived, Joseph Richards, and baptized these five converts. A year later, when war broke out in Burma and Major McCune's battalion of artillery was ordered to the front, he baptized his children who were of age before leaving.

After the war ended and Britain subjugated the Burmese empire, Major McCune decided to emigrate to Zion. He had been advised by President Nathaniel V. Jones of the India Mission to get out of India as soon as possible, for the judgments of God were soon to be poured out upon the inhabitants of that land. This prophecy was fulfilled.

The McCunes were unaccustomed to toil of any kind. In India they had hired servants by the dozens to wait on them. It was no small learning experience to drive ox teams, plow and weed fields, plant corn, cook over a campfire, fell trees and chop wood, mend and sew, cook and bake. But they pitched in every ounce of energy and muscle and no one heard a complaining word.

The McCunes lived near the Claridges and Alfred "was much taken up with Lizzette," and she had her eye on him. They had similar talents and qualities. As a young boy, Alfred had also entertained his schoolmates and friends during the long summer evenings. His friends would scamper to the steps of the meeting house with Alfred on the highest step. Elizabeth, Mary Ellen, Belle Park and numerous others of his age clustered close around where he stood. Each of them listened with anxious ears and glistening eyes to the stories or even fairy tales he'd gingerly and dramatically tell. His mother and father brought with them a number of exciting storybooks for their children.

As Mary Ellen said, "We little Nephites didn't have access to libraries or bookstores and were more than delighted to hear him tell what he had read."[10] His friends nicknamed him Alf and considered him "a wonderfully gifted storyteller." They were reluctant to leave for home until the tale was ended. Alfred had a good memory and a clear, pleasant voice. Often the stars were shining and during the full moon, the beautiful glow of the night lights added brilliance to the scene until they said goodnight.

How eagerly she and her friends looked forward to the periodic visits of their Prophet Brigham Young and his company. Everything was arranged for their comfort and entertainment. This was done as a labor of love. One of President Young's visits Elizabeth never forgot.

With bands playing music, many waving flags and banners, and she with her friends holding bouquets of flowers, they joyously went out to meet and greet their beloved leader. People were lined up on each side of the street waiting for the carriages to pass. Among them were Elizabeth and other young ladies dressed in white, who had strewn evergreens and flowers along the path. Soon the carriages arrived carrying the First Presidency of the Church, Brigham Young, Heber C. Kimball and Daniel H. Wells. As they emerged from their conveyances smiling with arms outstretched, they walked over the flowery path to be embraced by the Saints of Nephi. When Brother Kimball passed Elizabeth he said to her and four other girls dressed in white, "You five girls right here will live to be mothers in Israel."

Samuel Claridge, Elizabeth's father, invited the First Presidency and their wives to his home for dinner. How Elizabeth and her girlfriends flew around industriously to have everything nice for the "stylish city folks." As soon as the guests were seated for dinner the giggling girls slipped upstairs and tried on all the ladies' hats. To Elizabeth, "that was a real treat." She later said, "I venture to say that could the ladies have seen us next Sunday they would have been struck with the similarity of styles in Nephi and Salt Lake City millinery."[1]

The afternoon meeting held by President Young and his counselors was one Elizabeth would never forget. She and her friends dressed in white were given reserved seats in the front near the pulpit. The sermons were excellent and they were happy with the messages until the Prophet said he had the names of brethren called to be missionaries to go south with their families, and settle the "Muddy" (Moapa Valley, now in Nevada). Quite a large number of the men in Nephi had previously been called to settle the Dixie country along the Virgin River, but the "Muddy," so many miles farther south was so much more desolate—hot and forbidding. "Oh! Oh!" remembered Elizabeth, "I did not hear another name except Samuel Claridge." And then she burst into sobs and cried, paying no attention to her tears soiling her new white dress. The father of the teenage girl sitting next to Elizabeth was also called to go settle the "Muddy." Said she, "What are you crying about? It doesn't make me cry, I know my father won't go."

"Well, there's the difference," said Elizabeth, "I know that my father *will* go, and that nothing could prevent him, and I should not own him as a father if he would not go when called by the Prophet." Then she broke down sobbing again.

Misfortune and trouble beset Elizabeth's father to prevent him from getting off. When nearly ready to start, one of his horses got poisoned. He had to buy another horse. A week later one of his big mules was found choked to death in the barn. Some of the friends of the Claridges came to Samuel and declared rather firmly, "This shows you are not to go." But Elizabeth's father sternly replied, "It shows me that the adversary is trying to prevent me from going, but I shall go if I must walk."

The Claridges had moved into a new house and were fixed up very comfortably. Again Brother Claridges' friends tried to persuade him to keep the house and farm, go south to the "Muddy" for a while and then return to Nephi. Samuel Claridge knew this was not the kind of mission he had been called to fulfill. "I shall sell everything I own," he said, "and take my means to help build up another waste place in Zion."

Elizabeth's mother and sister remained in Nephi the

first year, but she and her brother accompanied their father. They packed their wagons and a year's supply of provisions. With Brother Harmon and his wife they traveled southward, camping at night under the stars, cooking their meals over a campfire to the accompaniment of song and laughter.

After two weeks of arduous travel, the Claridges and Harmons reached St. George. In the southern part of Utah Territory in the region called Utah's Dixie, the Indians were pillaging and molesting the white settlers. Just prior to the arrival of the "Muddy" missionaries, a number of people had been killed and others had their cattle and horses stolen. The Saints in St. George cautioned Brothers Claridge and Harmon not to travel to the "Muddy" except in a large caravan. The journey from St. George to the "Muddy," with loaded wagons, required three weeks' time.

They waited a week for more missionaries assigned to the "Muddy" to arrive in St. George, but none came. An Apostle of the Lord, Elder Erastus Snow, advised them to continue their journey. But what rough, winding, cobblestone-covered road they had to traverse! The scenery was lonely and barren, and following down the Virgin River were numerous quicksand pockets, enclosed on each side with towering mountains. The dismal echoes of the wagons from wall to wall suggested yelling Indians to ears strained to catch the first sound of the redman's war whoop. Each day became a horrible experience filled with haunting fear. Yet they pushed on. It was necessary to travel a certain number of miles each day to find suitable campgrounds.

Elizabeth had a remarkable gift of storytelling, so we shall tell some of the rest of their journey to the "Muddy" and many of her experiences in that wasteland (now part of the state of Nevada) in her own words. [2]

> One day I was riding in a wagon with my brother Sam; we were ahead of the others. Several times that day

I had made him stop his team because I thought I heard Indians. Each time it proved to be the shrill note of some wild bird. It was now sunset; we could see in the distance our camping place. My brother and I were singing and laughing when I suddenly heard a yell. "Sam," I said, "Stop the team! I heard the yell of an Indian."

"Yes, you have heard the same yell all day," he answered. I clutched him by the arm. "Stop, stop! I saw an Indian jump upon that rock and then jump back!" My brother stopped the team. The Indian stood up again and then bounded from one rock to another, followed by two others of his race. We waited until Father and Brother Harmon came up to us. By that time ten Indian warriors, all decked out in their war paint, were in sight. We stopped and held a solemn consultation. I shall never forget the words of my father, and the beautiful expression on his face, as he said:

"Don't be afraid, my children! We are in the hands of the Lord! He has called us on this mission. I have done everything in my power to fulfill it so far, and, therefore, our Father will see us through. Go right on; don't let the Indians think you are afraid, for there is nothing an Indian despises so much as cowardice!"

We drove right on to the camping place. There we found the Indians already camped. They had a whole band of horses with them, which were evidently the result of their plundering. As we approached they showed no sign of hostility. Father and Brother Harmon fed and watered our horses. Sam made a roaring campfire. By this time the moon was shining— it seemed to me as it never shone before. Eleven or twelve of the Indians came over to our camp and squatted peacefully around the fire. This was a sight which is forever rivetted on my mind.

Father shook hands with the Indians as they left us; then, after we had had our customary prayers, we all went quietly to bed. We pretended to sleep that night, but I think not one closed his eyes. I remember well the feeling of gratitude which came into my heart, when I thought, "What a good man my father is; our safety is due to his goodness and to the righteousness of Brother Harmon." They were both pure men and faithful Latter-day Saints. I felt secure as I reflected

that these two good men held that power which is the
Priesthood of God.

When we arose next morning we thanked our
Heavenly Father with overflowing hearts for protection during that perilous night. After breakfast we
gave the Indians a sack of flour and bade them all
goodbye. They shook my father's hand heartily and
said, "You good Mormons!"

Their next trouble was the Virgin River. Elizabeth
tells of the crooked winding course of the stream and
having to cross it many times. She relates the crossing
of quicksand. Were the teams to stop, the wagon would
sink quickly. Her father first drove his large strong pair
of mules hitched to the provision wagon. He glided
across, but Brother Harmon, not so expert in driving,
got his wagon stuck in the sucking quicksand bottom.
All three teams were quickly hitched to the Harmon
wagon and extricated it. At the next crossing Sister
Harmon refused to ride with her husband. "He does
not know how to drive," she scoffed.

Elizabeth's father invited, "Sister Harmon, you
come and ride with me." And Elizabeth reports, "Lo,
and behold, this time father got stuck." Not deridingly
but pleasantly Samuel Claridge declared, "Now we
know it is Sister Harmon who is the cause of our difficulty." The wagon was quickly sinking and all three
teams couldn't move it. Sister Harmon rode a horse out
of the river. She had never been on a horse's back
before. She was in tears and to her the experience was
tragic. But our heroic young lady Elizabeth tells us,
"Still the place resounded with my irresistible laughter." Then she continues her narrative:

It was a cold bleak morning, and the wind blew
fiercely: but the three men rolled up their pantaloons
and waded into the stream and carried every sack of
flour from the wagon to the shore. By the time everything was out, the wagon had sunk so deeply into the

sand that all the teams could hardly get it out. To cap
the climax the tongue broke. When the wagon was
finally out, poor father was so cold that he took a
severe chill. Hot drinks and good nursing soon
restored him, but it took the remainder of the day to
mend the wagon tongue.

The most difficult and torturous experience in all
their travels occurred the day before their intended
arrival at their destination in the "Muddy Valley."
Elizabeth relates it in her vividly descriptive style with
pathetic emotion.[3]

> We got up early in the morning and commenced to
> ascend Virgin Hill, which is over a mile long, and
> almost at the top is a huge rock which is almost per-
> pendicular. After having brought the wagons to this
> point by hitching three teams to each in succession,
> blocking the wheels at intervals while the horses rest-
> ed, our difficulties increased. As it was not possible for
> our horses to climb this steep rock, they were
> unhitched and led up the winding, narrow trail to the
> top of the rock. The horses were then hitched to a long
> heavy log chain which was dropped down and
> attached to the wagon. Then the horses pulled it up.
>
> This steep road was narrow; on either side was a
> precipice; the wagons must be kept in a straight line or
> they were apt to be dashed over the sides. To help
> matters the wind blew a perfect hurricane.
>
> The two light wagons went up all right. The heavy
> one was well on its way. My brother and I stood watch-
> ing the progress with grateful, happy hearts. But lo! a
> crash! The tongue that was broken in the river gave
> way and down came the wagon. As the massive thing
> dashed past me, it dragged my dress over the wheel.
> How narrow was my escape from being crushed to
> death! The wagon rolled down a ways, then suddenly
> plunged over the side of the precipice. Now it tumbled
> over and over, scattering the flour and other provisions
> all over the hillside. I shall never forget the look of con-

sternation on the faces of that group as they stood gaz-
ing at the destruction spread out below.

The scene was too much for my brother. He began
to abuse the country, and vowed that he would not go
another step to live in such a place. Poor boy, it was
discouraging. I was not daunted, however, and replied,
"Well, I shall. I wouldn't back out of this mission if
every one of the wagons tipped over." With a tremor in
his voice my brother said, "But look at your clothes."

My trunk happened to be in the wagon. I had been
the telegraph operator at Nephi for the past year or
two. My salary, though small, enabled me to buy some
good, comfortable clothes. In fact, I had a fine
wardrobe for a girl in those days.

"Yes," said he, "look at your trunk broken all to
pieces and your clothes blowing across the prairie!"
He thought if anything would touch a girl's heart it
would be that sight. But I snapped my fingers and
said, "I don't care that much for the old clothes."

My father had not spoken a word up to this point;
he now calmly turned to me and said, "My daughter, I
prophesy that the day will come, that you will have
much better clothes than those to wear." This prophecy,
as my friends can testify, has been fulfilled.

After gathering up all the things we could find,
and leaving one man with the wagon, the company
went on to the settlement. And oh, what a place it was!
Nothing but deep sand and burning sun. No houses,
only a few tents and dugouts. We all went to work
with a will, however, and at the end of one year we
had a nice farm of waving grain, and one nice large
adobe room to live in.[4]

Elizabeth carried every bucket of mortar, and every
adobe in this house to her father who laid up the walls.
Her brother hauled the adobes from where they were
made to the house site.

In later years after she and her husband and children lived in the mansion they built on the hillside in
Salt Lake City, some of her children attended the city

schools. One day a little playmate got angry with Elizabeth's little daughter, Jack, and insultingly said: "Miss Jack McCune, you needn't be so stuck up if you do live in a big house, for your mother used to make adobes." Jack was so horrified she couldn't believe what she heard. She flew into the mansion and demanded an explanation from her mother.

"Why, Jack," said her mother with a tantalizing smile, "Of course it's true. You see, my daughter, you have an uncommonly smart mother. Don't you think so? It isn't every little girl that has a mother who can make adobes."[5]

The valley of the Muddy River was a swamp of tules, scrubbrush, and wild hogs. It was hard to subdue. The main object for the call to the "Muddy" was to raise cotton for the people to make clothing. With the help of his son Sam, Samuel Claridge cleared several acres of land and planted cotton, grain, an orchard, and a vineyard. The pioneers on the "Muddy" met with hardships, privations, sickness, and death. Elizabeth said, "The tule swamps bred mosquitoes galore and we suffered with malaria. We dressed in homespun cotton colored with blue dyes. Our clothes and our faces were one color—we were blue with the chills."[6]

She remembered their first Thanksgiving. Her brother Sam shot a wild hog and Elizabeth prepared it for their dinner. The meat was white and sweet. The Claridge and Harmon families enjoyed it. The settlement they lived in was called St. Thomas. 150,000 pounds of ginned cotton was produced on the "Muddy."

The cotton pioneers on the "Muddy" stayed until February of 1872. A government survey that year proved the land was in Nevada. (At the time the Claridges and the other cotton missionaries settled in the valley of the "Muddy" they believed the land occupied was part of the territory of Utah.) Nevada demanded taxes be paid in gold and the cotton missionaries had no gold. President Brigham Young advised them to move back into the known territory of Utah. Elizabeth remembered: "As we could not sell anything, we left our houses standing empty and our beautiful crops unharvested."[7]

Most of the "Muddy" cotton missionaries went to Long Valley in Kane County. "Here my father lived in the United Order until it was abandoned," said Elizabeth. He was appointed first vice president of the Order and became one of the founders of Orderville.

Before her father left the "Muddy" Mission Elizabeth was brought to St. George on the solicitation of Elder Erastus Snow, president of the Southern Mission, to take charge of the telegraph office in St. George. The winter of 1871 she spent in St. George and took the leading parts in many stage plays in local theatricals. Her wit, unselfish good humor and charm of personality won the hearts of the people of St. George. Her excellent dramatic gifts and imagination were of inestimable value in all her later years, lending incisive delight and embellishing the bright web of her addresses in her public appearances among the daughters of Zion.

After a year in St. George, Elizabeth returned to Nephi on a visit and married her old sweetheart, Alfred W. McCune, the handsome, promising young son of Major Matthew McCune in the Endowment House in Salt Lake City in 1872. Happenings incident of a new country crammed the early years of their married life with exciting and thrilling events. Elizabeth relates one of the dangers that confronted the earlier settlers of the western frontier in which she was involved. Here it is:

> About three years after I was married I took my baby and traveled from Nephi to Long Valley on a visit to my parents. I started with Brother Stewart and his daughter Ella, and wrote for my father to meet me at a place called Ham's Ranch. When we got there my father had not arrived. Thinking he would soon come I stayed, and Brother Stewart went on to Kanab. The next morn-

ing he did not come, and then I knew he had missed the letter. Remembering that Brother Hoyt, of whom I was acquainted, had a sawmill somewhere in these mountains, I determined to go there. I told the people at the ranch if they would take me to Brother Hoyt's he would take me to my father. This one of the men did.

When we got to the mill we found Sister Hoyt and three little children alone. The men were a mile or two away cutting timber. She explained to me that the bishop had sent word for all the women folks to be moved into town as the Indians were threatening an outbreak. Some white men it seems had killed an Indian and they had sworn they would kill ten white men for revenge. Sister Hoyt concluded her story by saying, 'Yes, we are all ready to go to town tomorrow morning, and you can go with us.'

She had two bake kettles on the coals, in which two nice loaves of bread were baking. We sat there chatting without a thought of danger. I was telling her the Nephi news when the children ran in frightened and screaming, "Oh, mother, here is a band of Indians, they are coming right towards the house!"

There they were, mounted on horses and resplendent in their war paint and feathers. They were of the Navajo tribe; the very band that was making all the trouble. Well, there was nothing for us to do but face the situation. We were two weak women up in a canyon with no human aid within a mile. Imagine how we felt. I offered up a constant prayer in my heart to my Heavenly Father to preserve us from what might be worse than death.

They all came in, something over a dozen fierce warriors. I thought as they looked us over and then stood talking, "They are deciding what to do with us!" All at once I thought of the bread cooking on the fire and said, "Sister Hoyt, let us take these two nice loaves of hot bread and break it up and divide it among them." She answered, "All right." We then elbowed our way through the crowd of Indians, took the hot, steaming loaves from the kettle and proceeded to break them up. The Indians in the meanwhile closely watched our every movement. We asked them if they liked molasses on their bread. 'Yes,' they replied. Spreading each piece with molasses we passed them around. A perfect change came over the faces of the savages. They were pleased and showed it in every feature. Then we gave them a drink of water and they all shook hands with us saying, "Wyno squaw! Wyno squaw!" [i.e. "Good squaw"] and quietly took their departure.

With what fervency we thanked our Father for His protection and deliverance! When the men came home for supper, they did not complain because they had to eat mush and milk without bread that night.

I met my parents next morning, and as they had not received my letter, my arrival was a complete surprise.[11]

Elizabeth and Alfred with baby Fay lived but a short time in Nephi. Railroad building was spreading over the western country and mining of precious metals was popular. Alfred had developed into a preeminent organizer of human and physical forces, and was successfully involved in both. He was rapidly becoming a wealthy man with many enterprises. Elizabeth with her husband and child moved to Montana. Here Alfred formed a timber and mining business.

In 1898, after settling in Salt Lake City, Elizabeth was chosen a member of the General Board of the Young Women's Mutual Improvement Association. By then her children were mostly grown. She traveled extensively, inspiring, motivating and uplifting the lives of thousands of the young women of the Church. She attended with delight the duties given her, capably molding character into Saintly lives. Though wealthy and surrounded with luxury she never forgot the less fortunate.

She became a patron of the National Council of Women of the United States and of the International Council in 1899. Her travels all over the Church as a member of this board developed her natural powers of oratory infused by her innate tact and kindliness of spirit. Equal to every occasion she was as much at home on a rough wooden seat across a wagon box drawn by sweaty

horses over rough dusty roads in Idaho or Mexico—
"sweetening every difficulty with a smile and cheering all
discouraged hearts with her unfailing golden outlook on
life"—as she was in a palacious sleeping car. Beginning
with these years she became one of the most popular and
beloved figures amongst the women of Zion.[12]

When the Salt Lake Temple was completed and dedicated in 1893, she was chosen as a temple worker. She
continued as an ardent temple worker except when
absent from the state on other Church-assigned duties,
until the end of her mortal days. Her interest was centered with temple work and its closely associated
technical labor of research and ancestral record-making.
She consistently and faithfully sought after her own
kindred dead. In 1896 she sailed to England where she
gathered genealogy and visited relatives. While there
she turned her beautiful summer home in Eastbourne,
England, into headquarters for the Elders laboring in
that district, and invited them to make it their home
while serving their missions. She and her daughter,
Fay, accompanied the Elders to their street meetings
and helped them sing the songs of Zion which attracted
many passers-by to linger and listen to the missionaries'
message. Elizabeth and daughter, Fay, also enjoyed
going out tracting with the fulltime missionaries.

They attended Queen Victoria's jubilee, and at a
general gathering of curious English men and women
she testified of the virtuous womanhood of the
Mormon Church, refuting successfully numerous false-
hoods which had been circulated concerning the
deplorable condition of the women generally among
the Mormons. During her stay at Eastbourne, Elizabeth
was instrumental in converting two of her English relatives to the restored gospel of Jesus Christ.

The next year she made a return trip to Europe to
attend the International Congress of Women held in
London. At the close of the Congress sessions she, with

other members of the ICW, went to Windsor Castle, where they were royally entertained by Queen Victoria. Learning Elizabeth was a Mormon, her Majesty took her aside from the others and confided to her the interest she had in Mormonism and that she had read the Book of Mormon graciously presented to her by Elder Lorenzo Snow. This cheered the heart of our heroine who gave the Queen her solemn witness of the truth of Mormonism.

1905 was the year Elizabeth was appointed by Governor William Spry as a trustee of the Utah State Agriculture College at Logan. She served as a trustee for ten years, the last two years acting as Vice President of the Board with Lorenzo N. Stohl, President. While serving on that Board she toured the United States with her good friend Susa Young Gates, to investigate the home economic department in other colleges. Following her return and at her recommendation, a cafeteria was set up in Utah State Agriculture College and other improvements were established in the domestic science and art departments.

President Joseph F. Smith personally called her to serve as a member of the General Board of the Relief Society. Elizabeth's astute appraisal of human values, her philosophy and wise counsel, made her an invaluable member of that body of leading women. She traveled and preached the gospel, in her exquisitely delightful way, always bearing her firm testimony and cheering the Saints in every stake in the Church from Canada to Mexico and in almost all the missions, particularly those in Europe, Canada, and the Hawaiian Islands. She was ever ready to accept the hardest trips and face the difficulties from which others shrank. "As one of her friends expressed it, she was 'such a good sport.'" President Heber J. Grant observed, "It fell my lot upon many occasions to travel with her to different conferences and I know that there was no doubt whatever in her mind regarding the divinity of the work in which we as Latter-day Saints are engaged."[13]

Released from the Relief Society Board in 1920, Elizabeth was free to devote her whole time and energy to the work she loved the most, and which she considered more vitally important than any other, that pertaining to the salvation of the dead. Many were glad and willing to work for the living, but not so many would consecrate heart and soul to unselfish, persistent labor for the unseen spirits. She was appointed chairman of the Women's Committee for the Genealogical Society of Utah. With her beloved friend Susa Young Gates, she traveled once more over the Church, speaking on genealogy and temple work. She was an active participant in the International Congress of Genealogy held in San Francisco in 1915, during the World's Fair. She was a speaker at this convention, making the report of the women's committee of the Genealogical Society, and at that famous Genealogical Congress, she presented important lessons on how research of one's ancestors should be done.

Her voice was raised in all stakes in the Church with her marvelous gift of rousing interest, stimulating ambition and striking fire in the souls of her listeners. With the Spirit of God in her own heart she always left glad hearts behind her. As her only biographer, Susa Young Gates, averred, "She did more to popularize and extend the mission of the Genealogical Society than any other one labor that she performed during the last twenty years of her life."[14]

With Susa and other ladies she attended the International Council of Women at Rome. While in Europe she, with Susa, devoted time in searching out genealogical records in England, Germany, Norway, and Switzerland. While in London she joined Sister Stewart Eccles "in the beautiful work of tracting from house to house in the neighborhood of the mission headquarters." Elizabeth in clear, eloquent, and ofttimes witty speech, impressed many who came to the door, and a few were convinced of the truths she told them.

Between trips and in the midst of being a mother of nine grown sons and daughters, whom she tenderly loved, praying for their ultimate triumph in the truth of the Lord, she designed and with Alfred built one of the most magnificent homes ever erected in the entire western United States—a veritable palace upon "a heaven-kissed hill with spacious rooms, shadowed vistas and sweeping stairs." She used as her materials satins and tooled leather, woods laid down in rare South American forests for long months of seasoned worth; from Italian Carrara quarries came marbles of rose bloom, or pearl polished; artists from far-off eastern cities painted in her ceilings and panelled wall scenes from Sherwood forests. Priceless rugs from Persian looms lay on the floors or hung from the archways. "Given unlimited resources by her princely husband" she used the materials and artistry obtained to recreate a monument to harmony and exquisite architectural loveliness. In every corner, on every floor, from every ceiling and decorative wall, from all contours of the palace itself, the personality of the designer and builder is adorned—for Elizabeth was an artistic genius gifted with harmonious human self-expression.

During the years the McCunes lived in the mansion, many public and private functions were held there. The General and Stake officers of the Genealogical Society, the Relief Society and YWMIA Boards were lavishly entertained by the hostess and her family. Within the palace walls words of truth and prophecy were uttered by the prophets of her day. The spirit of peace and harmony permeated each room and rested upon each guest welcomed over the threshold.

One delightful private occasion in July 1917 was enjoyed by Elizabeth with her closest friends, Augusta W. Grant, Alice K. Smith, Ann D. Groesbeck, and Susa Young Gates, who were invited to a week's retreat within the spacious mansion. None of the husbands were invited. As each guest entered she was presented by the hostess with a lovely gingham gown. Each guest selected her own bedroom and bath. One of Elizabeth's guests wrote what they called a descriptive doggerel commemorative of the occasion.

> This is the house that Elizabeth built
> These are the women that Elizabeth asked
> To spend a week in the palace that she built.
> These are the dresses, all striped and fine
> That Elizabeth bought for the women that time
> To wear in the house that she built.

Elizabeth was called a philanthropist and surely she was. With Alfred's generous approval she was exceedingly generous and helpful. Through her influence her husband gave $5000 to the building of the Salt Lake Temple. To the Genealogical Library she gave $1000, and to save the Young Woman's Journal from folding up she contributed $500. These are only a few of the magnificent donations made by Elizabeth and Alfred to various worthy causes.

Though the wife of a rich mining man she was always a zealous Latter-day Saint and a lady highly and worthily esteemed. She was a faithful and devoted wife who shared with her husband poverty and hardship, and later, prosperity and wealth. She, with three of their children accompanied Alfred to Peru. He had connections with the Vanderbilts, the Morgans and the Hearsts. He purchased the famous Cerro de Pasco mines which had been worked by the Spaniards for the silver deposited there, but in the crudest possible manner, for over three hundred years. Alfred syndicated the mine and spent millions of dollars in purchasing and then developing the property. He built a railroad up into the cloud land, so high that the normal person's heart almost stops beating and it was difficult for ordinary people to get their breath. The development of this silver mine cost twenty million dollars before there were any returns from the mine.

By 1924 he was one of the chief owners in the mining company which became famous as one of the largest copper and silver mines in the world, producing each year the cost of the development. Yet Alfred retained genuine simplicity. He accepted success or failure with a smile, and with the sportsmanship that laughs at difficulties and dignifies poverty or riches as mere incidents in a busy life. Like his sweetheart of over fifty years, he maintained a keen sense of humor which made life for them an amusing pageant. Coupled with his humor was a stern probity and business integrity which paralleled his impatient contempt for chicanery or insincerity. His devotion and generosity to his family and his church was profuse and genuine. He acquired many friends and those who knew him best loved him most.

In 1920 Elizabeth and Alfred moved to California. Before their departure Elizabeth desired to give the palace on the heaven-blessed hill to the Church for use as the Authorities may decide. President Heber J. Grant, counselors, and Council of the Twelve graciously accepted the gift and turned the mansion over to the LDS School of Music. It was named the LDS McCune School of Music and Art in honor of its generous donors.

The spring of 1924 found Elizabeth with her husband in the Bermuda, but the climate and vegetation were uncongenial. Elizabeth's health broke down and she was prostrated. Enroute home to Salt Lake City she refused an operation in New York, and Alfred told her he'd take her to Zion and her people.

She lay on a bed in an upper east room of Hotel Utah, hopeful, cheerful and fully anticipating a complete recovery. Her thoughts dwelt on her husband, her children and once again having a home in the mountains of Zion. Her deep devotion for Alfred was evident in the love and patience which she manifested during all the years of their married life. She was a constant source of inspiration, comfort and encouragement to him and her children. She lay on her bed, peaceful and cheerful, happy when her dear husband and children were near, grateful when the Elders visited her sickroom and administered to her.

Until the last four days she clung to those who shared her unbounded confidence that God would extend her life on the earth to accomplish righteousness. But then one day with her friend, Susa Young Gates, who shared her unshaken faith for ultimate recovery, she begged to kneel by her bedside and tell the Lord in their joint prayer that they had given up and that she should be released to go to her heavenly home to enjoy eternal rest. Pneumonia set in and with comforting silence she died in the arms of her broken-hearted husband, surrounded by all her children.

In her death, in some ways, Elizabeth did as great a work as in her life. Quietly and unknown to anyone but Alfred, who gave glad assent to her wishes, she prepared a will which bequeathed $100,000 to forty-six relatives and friends, the Church and the Genealogical Society. Has there ever been, or will be, another woman so scrupulously mindful of others as she? She performed a work few men or women can equal.

Her funeral marked an epoch in Mormon society. It was the first time any woman except the four General Presidents of the Relief Society, had funeral services in the Assembly Hall, presided over by the Presidency of the Church. It was the first time that a woman's work with the struggling Genealogical Society had ever been publicly acknowledged and the work done by that Society honored. Her choice friend, Susa, was to pen: "Be sure her heart was glad as her spirit eyes looked about on that silent but nonetheless splendid miracle which her nobility, her meekness and her righteousness had wrought."[15]

Elizabeth Claridge McCune was one of the truly great women of the Church in these the latter days. She was great because of her philanthropies, because of her artistry and creative powers, which she was capable of releasing because of her own husband's lavish generosity. But most importantly of all, she was great because she built eternal ideals into the lives and characters of those about her, and she did it so gently and so modestly. What she was to her husband and family directly, she was indirectly to thousands of others.

No other woman in the latter days, in the writer's humble opinion, has ever climbed to such lofty height of service, of giving and of loving kindness, and reached such high positions as she, without losing one atom of genuine decorum, sweetness and unspoiled dignity. Such characteristics were coupled with firm faith in God and extensive work in building the kingdom of God on the earth. These are indispensable qualities of true greatness exemplified in the heroic woman, Elizabeth Claridge McCune.

She is at rest in a silent grave in Nephi where, when she was interred, the citizenry both old and young expressed their love and appreciation for a noble woman. Today few know of her or sing her praises. But by following the example of this heroic woman we, too, can influence for righteousness in these latter days.

Notes

[1] Susa Young Gates, *Memorial to Elizabeth Claridge McCune - Missionary, Philanthropist, Architect* (Salt Lake City: (publisher not listed), 1924), pp. 17-18.

[2] Andrew Jenson, *Latter-day Saint Biographical Encyclopedia,* (Salt Lake City), Vol. 2, p. 669.

[3] Gates, p. 21. All Elizabeth's narration quoted from Gates' *Memorial to Elizabeth Claridge McCune.*

[4] *Ibid.,* pp. 22-23.

[5] Susa Young Gates, *Elizabeth Claridge McCune* (Salt Lake City, Utah: Deseret News Press), Genealogical and Historical Magazine, Vols. 16-17, January 1925, p. 7.

6 James G. Bleak, *Annals of the Southern Mission,* typed copies in LDS Historians Library, Salt Lake City, Utah.

7 Gates, *Memorial,* p. 23.

8 B. H. Roberts, *A Comprehensive History of the Church, Century One* (Provo: Brigham Young University Press, 1965), Vol. IV, pp. 548-549.

9 *Utah Genealogical and Historical Magazine,* p. 1.

10 Gates, *op cit.,* p. 75.

11 Gates, *Ibid.,* p. 24-25.

12 Gates, *Ibid.,* p. 27.

13 Gates, *Ibid.,* p. 60.

14 *Ibid.,* p. 28.

15 Gates, in *Utah Genealogical and Historical Magazine,* Vols. 16 and 17, p. 12.

The Patriarchal Office

The little apartment above the Whitney store in Kirtland was the scene of many profound events, including the School of the Prophets, meetings of the brethren, sacred visions and revelations, and ordinances. The purpose and the organization of the Church were being defined. It became clear that the Church was to be directed under the same order as was outlined by Paul in the New Testament, with apostles, prophets, evangelists, deacons, teachers, and priests. Joseph Smith, Sr., was called to be the evangelist, or presiding patriarch, to the Church.[46] On 18 December 1833, Joseph blessed his father and set him apart to this office. He and his counselors, Sidney Rigdon and Frederick G. Williams, laid their hands on Father Smith's head and ordained him. Oliver Cowdery wrote the blessings as they were given.

A year after this ordination, on 9 December 1834, Father Smith, acting in his office as Church Patriarch, gave blessings to Joseph and Emma.

Patriarchal Blessings

Patriarchal blessings are most sacred and personal to the one receiving them. The Prophet Joseph, as head of the dispensation of the fullness of times, and Emma, as his wife, hold a particularly personal relationship to every soul who embraces the gospel. Because of this, these precious documents do not belong only to their direct descendants; they belong to all.

Joseph's patriarchal blessing gives a glimpse into the place he holds in the eternal scheme of things, as head of the last dispensation. It also sheds some light upon what was being hinted at in the 1830 revelation to Emma, when she was told to rejoice in the "glory" that was to come upon her husband. Although it may seem that Emma is consigned to a reflected glory, the position she holds as wife of the Prophet Joseph Smith is glorious and encompasses great responsibility, both for herself and for her posterity. Both of these blessings define the glorious responsibility of the Prophet and his wife and, especially in the case of Joseph's blessing, transcend mortal expectations. In it we find out a great deal about the biblical Joseph, who was sold into Egypt; we better understand the hopes this Joseph had for the future, knowing that in the latter days, he would have a namesake who would fulfill a divine mission. Whereas Joseph of old provided grain to save a starving Israel, the latter-day prophet Joseph would provide sustenance for the soul. Through him the gathering of latter-day Israel would be accomplished, whether from mortal toil or by his sustaining effort from beyond the veil.

The inclusion of these blessings here provides one of the rare occasions for us to read words spoken personally by Joseph Sr.

Joseph's Patriarchal Blessing

Joseph Smith, My son, I lay my hands upon thy head in the name of the Lord Jesus Christ, to confirm upon thee a father's blessing. The Lord thy God has called thee by name out of the heavens. Thou hast heard his voice from on high, from time to time, even in thy youth. The hand of the angel of his presence has been extended toward thee, by which thou hast been lifted up and sustained; yea, the Lord has delivered thee from the hands of thine enemies; and thou hast been made to rejoice in his salvation: thou hast sought to know his ways, and from thy childhood thou hast meditated much upon the great things of his law. Thou hast suffered much in thy youth, and the poverty and afflictions of thy father's family have been a grief to thy soul. Thou hast desired to see them delivered from bondage, for thou hast loved them with a perfect love. Thou hast stood by thy Father, and . . . would have covered his nakedness rather than see him exposed to shame; when the daughters of the gentiles laughed, thy heart has been moved with a just anger to avenge thy kindred. Thou hast been an obedient son and the commands of thy Father, and the reproofs of thy mother, thou has respected and obeyed—for all of these things the Lord my God will bless thee. Thou hast been called, even in thy youth to the great work of the Lord, to do a work in this generation which no other man would do as thyself, in all things according to the will of the Lord. A marvelous work and a wonder has the Lord wrought by thy hand, even that which shall prepare the way for the remnants of his people to come in among the gentiles, with their fullness, as the tribes of Israel are restored. I bless thee with the blessings of thy forefathers, Abraham, Isaac, and Jacob; . . .

CONTINUED IN